Learning
MANDARIN
CHINESE
CHARACTERS

VOLUME 1

YI REN

TUTTLE Publishing

Tokyo | Rutland, Vermont | Singapore

About Tuttle
"Books to Span the East and West"

Our core mission at Tuttle Publishing is to create books which bring people together one page at a time. Tuttle was founded in 1832 in the small New England town of Rutland, Vermont (USA). Our fundamental values remain as strong today as they were then—to publish best-in-class books informing the English-speaking world about the countries and peoples of Asia. The world has become a smaller place today and Asia's economic, cultural and political influence has expanded, yet the need for meaningful dialogue and information about this diverse region has never been greater. Since 1948, Tuttle has been a leader in publishing books on the cultures, arts, cuisines, languages and literatures of Asia. Our authors and photographers have won numerous awards and Tuttle has published thousands of books on subjects ranging from martial arts to paper crafts. We welcome you to explore the wealth of information available on Asia at **www.tuttlepublishing.com.**

Published by Tuttle Publishing, an imprint of Periplus Editions (HK) Ltd

www.tuttlepublishing.com

Copyright © 2016 Periplus Editions (HK) Ltd
Front cover photo © takayuki/Shutterstock.com
Photo page 6: Wikimedia Commons

ISBN: 978-0-8048-4491-8

Distributed by

North America, Latin America & Europe
Tuttle Publishing
364 Innovation Drive
North Clarendon,
VT 05759-9436 U.S.A.
Tel: 1 (802) 773-8930
Fax: 1 (802) 773-6993
info@tuttlepublishing.com
www.tuttlepublishing.com

Asia Pacific
Berkeley Books Pte. Ltd.
61 Tai Seng Avenue, #02-12
Singapore 534167
Tel: (65) 6280-1330
Fax: (65) 6280-6290
inquiries@periplus.com.sg
www.periplus.com

21 20 19 18   10 9 8 7 6 5 4 3
Printed in Singapore   1809MP

Contents

10 Let's Go Shopping! 走，买东西去！

11 Do You Like to Eat Fruits? 你喜欢吃水果吗？

12 He Loves His Dog! 他很爱他的小狗！

Some Tips on Learning
Mandarin Chinese Characters

Look at the nature surrounding you, the mountains, the rivers, the trees, the flowers, the animals and the people. All have different shapes and different voices. Ancient Chinese people living within this beautiful world found a unique way for humans to communicate with each other. They created the Chinese characters!

From oracle-bone script to bronze inscriptions, from seal script to clerical script, from regular script to simplified Chinese characters, centuries upon centuries have passed by and those square shaped figures are still being used by a vast population today.

Chinese characters from past to present

There are two other ancient writing systems known to man, the Sumerian cuneiform and the Egyptian hieroglyphs. Of the three, the Chinese character writing system is the only ancient writing system still being used today. Credit for this goes to several distinct features that make Chinese characters unique.

Three Basic Elements of the Chinese Character: Form, Sound and Meaning
汉字的三个基本要素: 形, 音, 义

Chinese characters are known as square shaped characters. Each character is made up of three basic elements: form, sound and meaning. For example,

"我" is the form.
"**wǒ**" is the sound.
"I" is the meaning.

Over time, there have been many changes in the phonetics of Chinese characters. The composition and meanings, however, have remained somewhat the same. As a result, many Chinese people today can read ancient texts without much difficulty.

Before the inception of Chinese characters, communication was difficult within China due to the number of vastly different dialects being spoken. Chinese characters gave people a common ground for understanding.

One Syllable and Single Characters
单音节和独体字

Chinese characters are single characters with one syllable. These characters are created by drawing pictures of objects. Over time the characters have evolved from pictures into symbols. The symbols were standardized, then simplified to make writing easier. This simplified version is very basic in structure. It can't be divided into components or radicals. For example,

月 **yuè** means "moon"
木 **mù** means "tree" or "wood"
山 **shān** means "mountain"
水 **shuǐ** means "water"

Many of these types of characters are classified as Chinese "pictograms."

In addition, there is another small category of characters that are direct iconic illustrations. Examples of these include:

上 **shàng** for "up" and 下 **xià** for "down".

These were originally a dot above and below a line. Single number characters, such as,

一 **yī** for "one"
二 **èr** for "two"
三 **sān** for "three"

are also included in this category.

Composed Characters with New Meanings
具有新义的合体字
In the Chinese language there are many compound characters. Compound characters are made up of two or more single characters. When single characters are joined, the meaning and pronunciation of the character can change dramatically. There are twelve ways to compose Chinese characters. For example,

from top to bottom: 日 + 生 = 星
from left to right: 其 + 月 = 期
from left to middle to right:
言(讠) + 身 + 寸 = 谢 and so on.

Here are two frequently used ways to compose compound characters.

1) Two single characters may be combined to create a new single character with a new meaning.

木	+	交	➡	校
wood		cross, hand over		school

女	+	子	➡	好
woman		son, seed		good

2) Two single characters may be joined to form a new word. This new word is pronounced by speaking the individual characters, one after the other. The definition of this newly formed word may be similar to the individual original definitions or it may be completely changed. Look carefully at the following examples.

飞	+	机	➡	飞机
fly		machine, plane		plane, aircraft
读	+	书	➡	读书
read		book		read book
关	+	系	➡	关系
close, shut	system, series			relationship

In this book, you will see that many compound characters are composed in these two ways.

Various Radicals　多样化的偏旁部首
A Chinese radical (or "section header") is sometimes considered a "classifier." It is a particular component of most compound characters that can be found in various positions within the word. The radical usually gives a clue as to the meaning of the character. It can also help with the pronunciation of a word. Characters with the same radical can be grouped together for the easy of studying or used as a point of reference for indexing. The Chinese dictionary is a great example of this.

As you look through this book, you will find that Chinese characters, such as 吗, 吃, 妈, 她, the 口 and 女 are called radicals. You may wonder how or why a single character, such as 口 or 女, can become a radical. The answer is this: When compound characters are composed of two single characters, one of those characters becomes the radical. You can see it here in 吗, 吃, 妈, and 她.

Radicals, such as 口 and 女 keep their original single character form, but their shape may be narrowed or shortened. Many character components are distorted or changed in order to fit within the block shape alongside other characters. Some words or characters may take on a different shape completely. For example,
人 turns to 亻 as a radical for 你, 他, and 们.
言 changes to 讠 as a radical for 说, 话, and 读.
水 becomes 氵 as a radical for 沙, 河, and 湖.
These are only a few examples to give you a general idea.

For many years, Chinese dictionaries have contained more than 200 radicals. You will easily be able to memorize the list of commonly used radicals offered here. They appear often in this book.

Some Commonly Used Chinese Radicals

Radicals 偏旁部首	Examples 字例	Radicals 偏旁部首	Examples 字例
亻	你，他，们	宀	家，字，宝
女	妈，姐，她	口	吃，喝，唱
讠	说，话，语	日	明，昨，晴
氵	汉，河，漂	阝	那，都，院
纟	红，绿，纱	辶	这，边，还
木	样，校，椅	艹	茶，苹，菜

Chinese radicals appear in various positions within the word or character. Some radicals appear on the left side of the character 你, 他, 们, while other radicals appear on the right side of the character 都, 那, 邓. Some radicals appear at the top of a character 茶, 菜, 花, while other radicals appear at the bottom of a character 名, 合, 右. In general, semantic components tend to appear at the top or on the left side of character, while phonetic components tend to appear at the bottom or on the right side of character. As you learn more Chinese characters, you will learn to recognize the radicals in their various positions. Recognizing the radicals will also help you increase your vocabulary quickly.

The Strokes of Chinese Characters
汉字的笔画

When you use a pencil, pen or brush to draw pictures, you draw lines, circles or curves, one step at a time. When you use a pencil, pen or brush to write Chinese characters, you make lines, dots or hooks, one step at a time. The principles for drawing pictures and writing Chinese characters are very much the same. Far from being complicated, Chinese characters are simple drawings made from simple strokes. There are about thirty strokes in all. Among them are eight basic strokes that form the core and are used most often. All strokes have their own name and particular method of formation.

See the table below containing the eight basic strokes and how to form them.

Eight Basic Strokes and Method of Formation

Stroke 笔画	Name 名称	Writing direction 书写方向	Writing instruction 写法要点	Examples 字例
一	horizontal stroke 横 / héng	written from left to right	horizontal with the right end slightly up	二
丨	vertical stroke 竖 / shù	written from top to bottom	straight from top to bottom	十
丿	downward-left stroke 撇 / piě	written from top right to bottom left	start with force, end slightly	人
乀	downward-right stroke 那 / nà	written from top left to bottom right	start with force, pull to the right in the end	大
丶	dot 点 / diǎn	written from top to bottom right or left	dot to lower right or left, then pause	学
ノ	upward stroke 提 / tí	written from bottom left to top right	to upper-right, thinner at the end	习
亅	hook stroke 勾 / gōu	vertical stroke with a hook	a vertical line with a tiny rising tip at the end	小
ㄱ	turning stroke 折 / zhé	horizontal stroke with a vertical downturn	horizontal stroke, turn to the right down in vertical	口

Learn to recognize and become familiar with each individual stroke. Its name, writing direction and correct formation are all important. Whether the character is simple or complex, comprised of just a few strokes or many, the construction of each Chinese character relies heavily upon correct stroke formation. By focusing on the individual strokes, you will also be memorizing the character.

Stroke Order and Rules
笔画顺序规则

Throughout the years, rules have developed for writing Chinese characters. These rules help in learning the correct formation of characters. It doesn't matter whether you are right handed or left handed. If you follow the rules for stroke order, you will be able to write beautiful Chinese characters.

Here are the main stroke order rules for forming Chinese characters. These general rules will help you understand more specific stroke order rules later on.

1) Stroke from top to bottom

三	three	page 11
点	dot	page 34

2) Stroke from left to right

你	you	page 17
他	he	page 17

3) Stroke from the horizontal before vertical

下	under	page 36
工	work	page 85

4) Stroke from the horizontal before the down stroke to the left

在	exist, be, at	page 39
有	have, has	page 70

5) Stroke from the down stroke to left before to the right

师	teacher	page 52
朋	friend	page 77

6) The enclosing strokes first, then the enclosed and finally the sealing stroke

四	four	page 12
日	sun, date	page 38

7) The middle stroke before those on both sides

水	water	page 106
小	small	page 68

8) Left-falling stroke before right-falling stroke

八	eight	page 13
今	present	page 35

Following these simple rules will help you write any character you desire. Just remember to form the strokes correctly and in the right order from the very start. Otherwise you will find yourself repeating the same mistakes without knowing it. Correct stroke formation and stroke order will become more critical as your Chinese characters become more complex.

The Philosophy of Writing Chinese Characters
书写汉字的哲学

What is the philosophy behind writing Chinese characters? The philosophy can be summed up in one simple word: Balance!

Balance means, the writer needs to remain calm in emotion and thought, focused on the character and follow the rules of stroke formation and stroke order. Remember to place the strokes evenly throughout (top to bottom, left to right, horizontal to vertical, and so on).

Take a look at these characters:

山, 水 and 朋 are balanced from left to right;
早, 果 and 召 are balanced from and top to bottom;
国, 园 and 围 are balanced from outside to inside.

Each character appears to be accurate, well balanced and will look beautiful on paper.

Imagine drawing a person with a big head and small legs. Or a person with one arm longer than the other. The drawing would not look right. It would not look good. It might even look as though the picture could tip over or fall down. In any case, it would not look balanced. In that same way, if you write a character with longer strokes on the left and shorter strokes on the right, it won't look balanced either. It won't look accurate. It won't look good

9

on paper. For example, look at the character 山 **shān** "mountain." The center stroke is the longest, which represents the top of the mountain. Both sides contain vertical strokes which are the same in length. Thus, the character 山 is balanced. It looks accurate. It looks good on paper. If the left vertical stroke were longer than the right vertical stroke, the 山 "mountain" may appear off center or off balance. It may look as though the mountain could crumble to the ground.

In short, keep this simple word in mind when writing Chinese characters: "Balance!"

Enjoy Your Handwriting
祝你愉快地学写汉字

The same philosophy is true for both daily life and writing Chinese letters. Balance is the key. To keep this in mind will give you happy feeling when you practice your Chinese characters using this book. This book is for all people everywhere and at all levels. It can be used by youth or students who want to learn and practice writing Chinese characters on their own. It can also be used by people who are preparing to take the HSK Level 1 exam and as a foundation of AP Chinese exam. All characters and composed words are chosen from the HSK Level 1 exam. These characters and words are essential for studying the Chinese language. (The HSK exam is a Chinese Proficiency Test or Chinese Standard Exam for all non-Chinese speakers. The HSK exam is similar to the TOEFL exam for non-English speakers. The difference between the two is, the HSK exam has six test levels.)

Once you begin work in this book, you will find that following the step by step stroke order makes writing Chinese characters simple and easy. Use the space provided to practice writing on your own. In addition to writing individual characters, you will soon be able to write composed words and complete the practice exercises.

Each set of practice exercise is designed to reinforce, as well as extend, the learner's knowledge. You will quickly become very familiar with the vast number of Chinese characters offered here. You will know how to form Chinese characters and use them properly. There are twelve exercises in all. Each practice exercise is a culmination of material covered. For your convenience, an Answer Key is provided in the back of the book.

On each page with a featured Chinese character, you will find step by step stroke order directions which are easy to follow. You will also find three vocabulary words, phrases or idioms which relate to that featured Chinese character. Those phrases, idioms and proverbs are particularly well known in China and used in written, as well as oral language.

An index with English, Chinese characters and Pinyin is also provided in the back of this book. It is arranged in alphabetical order, making it easier for English speakers to search for Chinese characters.

As previously mentioned, all characters in this book are written in the simplified Chinese style. This is due to the fact that most people use this format. Today, Chinese writing is horizontal and moves from left to right, as in English. But in the past, Chinese writing was vertical and went from top to bottom, right to left.

As in art, you will find a sense of joy and accomplishment in creating beautiful Chinese characters. As you look at the characters you created with your own hand, you will be motivated to write even more. This process of handwriting stimulates many parts of your brain. It improves your memory, as well as your creativity. I truly hope that you find the practice of writing Chinese characters a joyous and rewarding experience.

Yi Ren

I would like to express my appreciation to my editor, June Chong, for her professional advice; to my friends Karen Enos for her proof-reading and editorial suggestions; Jie Ding who checked the accuracy of Chinese characters; Yang-yang Li who helped prepare the index and to my husband Suisheng Zhao who supported me. Thank you all for your help with this project!

	yī one	**common words** 一年　**yīnián**　one year 一月　**yīyuè**　January 一叶知秋　**yí yè zhī qiū**　(lit.) the falling of 　　one leaf heralds the coming of autumn	**radical** 一
一 (1 stroke)			

一	一	一	一							

	èr two	**common words** 二月　**èryuè**　February 二胡　**èrhú**　erhu (Chinese musical instrument) 二者必居其一　**èrzhě bì jū qíyī**　either one 　　or the other	**radical** 一
二 (2 strokes)			

二	二	二	二	二						

	sān three	**common words** 三月　**sānyuè**　March 三角形　**sānjiǎoxíng**　triangle 三五成群　**sān wǔ chéngqún**　in small 　　groups	**radical** 一
三 (3 strokes)			

三	三	三	三	三	三					

四	**sì** four	**common words**	radical
(5 strokes)		四月　**sìyuè**　April 四季　**sìjì**　four seasons 四面八方　**sìmiàn bāfāng**　in all directions; 　　　all around	口

丨	冂	冋	四	四	四	四	四			

五	**wǔ** five	**common words**	radical
(4 strokes)		五月　**wǔyuè**　May 五味　**wǔwèi**　all sorts of flavors 五颜六色　**wǔ yán liù sè**　multiple colors; 　　　colorful	一

一	丆	五	五	五	五	五				

六	**liù** six	**common words**	radical
(4 strokes)		六月　**liùyuè**　June 六年　**liùnián**　six years 六六大顺　**liù liù dàshùn**　everything is 　　　going smoothly	亠

丶	亠	六	六	六	六	六				

七	**qī** seven	**common words**	
(2 strokes)		七月　**qīyuè**　July 七百　**qībǎi**　seven hundred 七上八下　**qī shàng bā xià**　be agitated; 　in an unsettled state of mind	radical 一

一　七　七　七　七

八	**bā** eight	**common words**	
(2 strokes)		八月　**bāyuè**　August 八成　**bāchéng**　eight percent 八面玲珑　**bāmiàn línglóng**　be smooth 　and slick (in establishing social relations)	radical 八

丿　八　八　八　八

九	**jiǔ** nine	**common words**	
(2 strokes)		九月　**jiǔyuè**　September 九天　**jiǔtiān**　nine days 九牛一毛　**jiǔniú yīmáo**　(lit.) one hair from 　nine oxen; (fig.) a drop in the ocean	radical 丿

丿　九　九　九　九

十	**shí** ten	**common words**		radical
(2 strokes)		十月　**shíyuè**　October 十字架　**shízìjià**　cross 十全十美　**shí quán shí měi**　to be perfect		十

一	十	十	十	十							

零	**líng** zero	**common words**		radical
(13 strokes)		零食　**língshí**　snack 零钱　**língqián**　small change 零七八碎　**líng qī bā suì**　be scattered and 　　　disorderly		雨

一	二	户	雨	雨	雨	雨	雨	雩	雯	雯	
零	零	零	零	零							

1. Read the pinyin. Then write the numbers in Chinese characters.

yī	èr	sān	sì	wǔ

liù	qī	bā	jiǔ	shī	líng

2. Fill in the table using pinyin and Chinese characters.

English	Pinyin	Chinese characters
fifteen	shíwǔ	十五
twenty two		
thirty seven		
nineteen		
sixty eight		
seventy one		
eighty four		

3. Fill in the brackets with the correct number.

六 (**6**)　　　七 ( )　　　三 ( )　　　九 ( )

五 ( )　　　四 ( )　　　八 ( )　　　十 ( )

零零七 ( )　　　五十二 ( )　　　八十三 ( )

九十九 ( )　　　四十四 ( )　　　五十五 ( )

七十七 ( )　　　八十八 ( )　　　六十六 ( )

十二 ( )　　　三十一 ( )　　　七十六 ( )

4. Match the numbers to the corresponding Chinese characters.

twelve	三十一	ninety two	五十六
二十六	fifty six	六十五	forty eight
thirty one	fourteen	eighty nine	七十三
十二	四十八	seventy three	九十二
八十九	twenty six	十四	sixty five

| 我 (7 strokes) | **wǒ** I, me | **common words** 我们　**wǒmen**　we; us 自我　**zìwǒ**　self 我行我素　**wǒxíng wǒ sù**　to do things in one's own way | **radical** 戈 |

| 你 (7 strokes) | **nǐ** you | **common words** 你好　**nǐhǎo**　hello 你对了　**nǐduìle**　you are right 你追我赶　**nǐ zhuī wǒ gǎn**　try to overtake each other in friendly emulation | **radical** 亻 |

| 他 (5 strokes) | **tā** he | **common words** 其他　**qítā**　other 他人　**tārén**　other people 他乡遇故知　**tāxiāng yù gùzhī**　meeting an old friend in a foreign place | **radical** 亻 |

17

她	**tā** she	**common words**		radical 女
(6 strokes)		她们 **tāmen** they 她的 **tāde** hers 她家 **tājiā** her home		

亻	女	女	如	如	她	她	她	她		

们	**men** person (to form plural) 們 Traditional	**common words**		radical 亻
(5 strokes)		咱们 **zánmen** we; us 女士们 **nǚshìmen** ladies 先生们 **xiānshēngmen** gentlemen		

丿	亻	亻	们	们	们	们	们			

很	**hěn** very	**common words**		radical 彳
(9 strokes)		很远 **hěnyuǎn** very far 很近 **hěnjìn** very near 很多 **hěnduō** a lot of		

亻	彳	彳	彳	彳	很	很	很	很	很	很
很										

好	hǎo good	**common words**	
(6 strokes)		好人　**hǎorén**　good person 好吃　**hǎochī**　delicious 好事多磨　**hǎoshì duōmó**　good things 　　　　don't come easy	radical 女

叫	jiào call, shout	**common words**	
(5 strokes)		叫车　**jiàochē**　call for a car 叫座　**jiàozuò**　draw a large audience 叫苦连天　**jiàokǔ liántiān**　complain 　　　　endlessly	radical 口

什	shén what	**common words**	
(4 strokes)		什么　**shénme**　what 什么的　**shénmede**　and so on 什么店　**shénmediàn**　what store	radical 亻

么	**me** interrogative particle 麼 Traditional	**common words** 怎么 **zěnme** how 这么 **zhème** in this way 为什么 **wèishénme** why	**radical** 厶

(3 strokes)

么	么	么	么	么	么				

名	**míng** name	**common words** 名字 **míngzi** name 名牌 **míngpái** famous brand 名胜古迹 **míngshèng gǔjì** historical sites and scenic spots	**radical** 夕

(6 strokes)

丿	夕	夕	夕	名	名	名	名	名	

字	**zì** character, word	**common words** 字典 **zìdiǎn** character dictionary 字体 **zìtǐ** form of a written character 字里行间 **zìlǐ hángjiān** (idiom) between the lines	**radical** 宀

(6 strokes)

丶	丷	宀	宁	字	字	字	字	字	

高 (10 strokes)	**gāo** high, tall	**common words** 高兴 **gāoxìng** happy; joyful 高速 **gāosù** high speed 高山流水 **gāoshān liúshuǐ** (lit.) lofty mountains and flowing water	radical 亠

高 亠 立 立 亡 亡 冎 高 高 高 高

高 高

兴 (6 strokes)	**xìng/xīng** mood 興 Traditional	**common words** 兴奋 **xīngfèn** be excited 兴趣 **xìngqù** interest 兴高采烈 **xìng gāo cǎi liè** cheerful; in great spirits	radical 八

丷 丷 丷 兴 兴 兴 兴 兴

认 (4 strokes)	**rèn** recognize 認 Traditional	**common words** 认为 **rènwéi** think 认真 **rènzhēn** serious 认识 **rènshi** to know; recognize	radical 讠

讠 讠 认 认 认 认 认

| 识 (7 strokes) | **shí** know 識 Traditional | **common words** 识字　**shízì**　be able to read 识别　**shíbié**　identify 识时务者为俊杰　**shíshíwù zhě wéi jùnjié** whoever understands the times is a great man | radical 讠 |

| 吗 (6 strokes) | **ma** question particle 嗎 Traditional | **common words** 对吗？　**duìma**　Is it right? 是吗？　**shìma**　Is it? Is that so? 真的吗？　**zhēndema**　Really? | radical 口 |

| 呢 (8 strokes) | **ne** question particle | **common words** 你呢　**nǐne**　how about you 忙着呢　**mángzhene**　busy 管他呢　**guǎntāne**　whatever | radical 口 |

WORD PRACTICE

我们 **wǒmen** we, us

我	们								

什么 **shénme** what

什	么								

名字 **míngzi** name

名	字								

高兴 **gāoxìng** happy, joyful

高	兴								

认识 **rènshi** to know, recognize

认	识								

怎么 **zěnme** how

怎	么								

1. Write the appropriate Chinese characters in the brackets.

good   (   )   very good   (   )   I   (   )

we   (   )   you—singular   (   )   you—plural   (   )

he   (   )   they   (   )   she   (   )

they   (   )   call   (   )   name   (   )

2. Read the pinyin. Write each sentence in Chinese characters.

1)   **nǐhǎo ma? wǒ hěn hǎo, nǐne?**

_____

2)   **nǐ jiào shénme míngzi?**

_____

3)   **tā jiào shénme míngzi?**

_____

4)   **hěn gāoxìng rènshi nǐ.**

_____

3. Identify the characters with the same radicals. Then write the characters in the space provided.

我	好	叫	他
什	你	呢	高
吗	名	她	识
兴	们	很	字

人（亻）＿＿＿＿　＿＿＿＿　＿＿＿＿　＿＿＿＿

她（女）＿＿＿＿　＿＿＿＿

口（口）＿＿＿＿　＿＿＿＿　＿＿＿＿

4. Link the radical in the left column to the appropriate right character to form a new word.

亻	人	他
讠	也	
彳	口	
夕	子	
宀	艮	

5. Choose the right character to make compound words.

rèn	hěn	xìng	shén	men	zì	ne
认	很	兴	什	们	字	呢

高＿＿＿＿＿　　＿＿＿＿识　　＿＿＿＿好

我＿＿＿　　＿＿＿么　名＿＿＿　　你＿＿＿

25

6. Rearrange the word order to form correct sentences.

1) 你名什字么叫？

_____

2) 你认她吗识？

_____

3) 他兴很高。

_____

4) 认你高识很兴。

_____

7. Write each sentence in Chinese characters.

1) How are you?

_____

2) I am fine, and you?

_____

3) It is nice to meet you!

_____

谢	xiè thank	**common words**	
		感谢 **gǎnxiè** appreciate; grateful	radical 讠
(12 strokes)	謝 Traditional	谢谢 **xièxie** thank you; thanks 谢天谢地 **xiè tiān xiè dì** Thank heavens!	

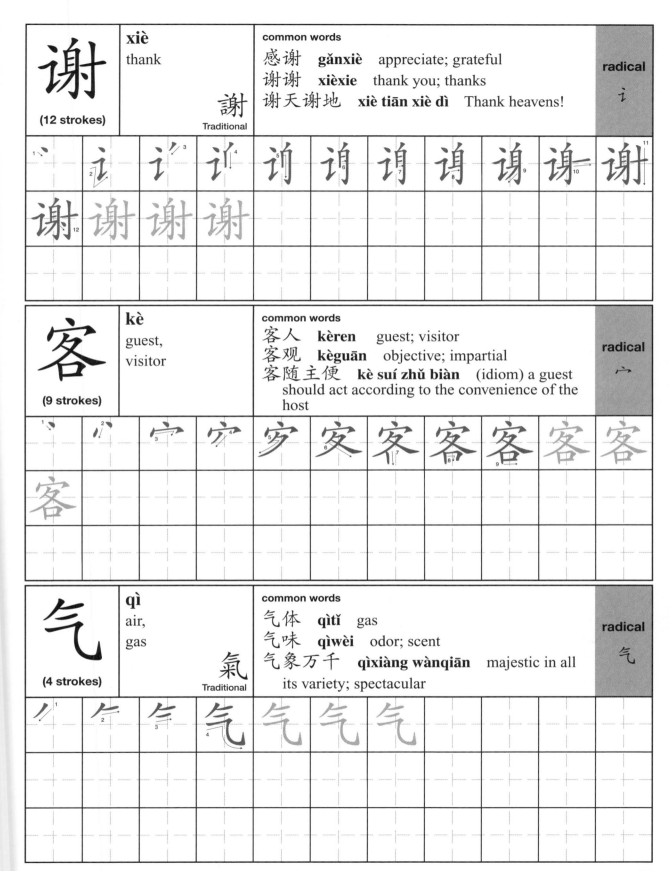

客	kè guest, visitor	**common words**	
		客人 **kèren** guest; visitor	radical 宀
(9 strokes)		客观 **kèguān** objective; impartial 客随主便 **kè suí zhǔ biàn** (idiom) a guest should act according to the convenience of the host	

气	qì air, gas	**common words**	
		气体 **qìtǐ** gas	radical 气
(4 strokes)	氣 Traditional	气味 **qìwèi** odor; scent 气象万千 **qìxiàng wànqiān** majestic in all its variety; spectacular	

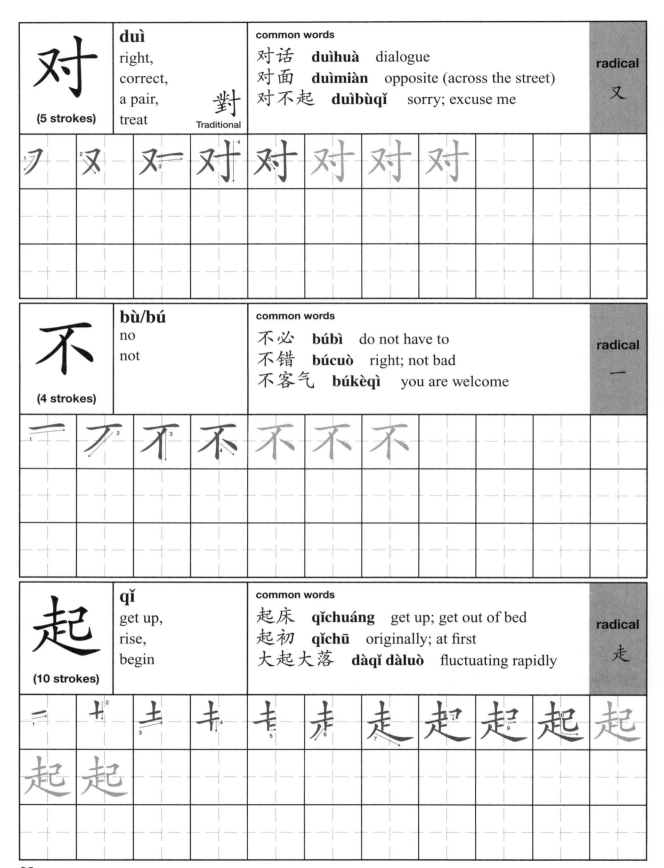

对	duì	common words	radical
(5 strokes)	right, correct, a pair, treat 對 Traditional	对话 **duìhuà** dialogue 对面 **duìmiàn** opposite (across the street) 对不起 **duìbùqǐ** sorry; excuse me	又

不	bù/bú	common words	radical
(4 strokes)	no not	不必 **búbì** do not have to 不错 **búcuò** right; not bad 不客气 **búkèqì** you are welcome	一

起	qǐ	common words	radical
(10 strokes)	get up, rise, begin	起床 **qǐchuáng** get up; get out of bed 起初 **qǐchū** originally; at first 大起大落 **dàqǐ dàluò** fluctuating rapidly	走

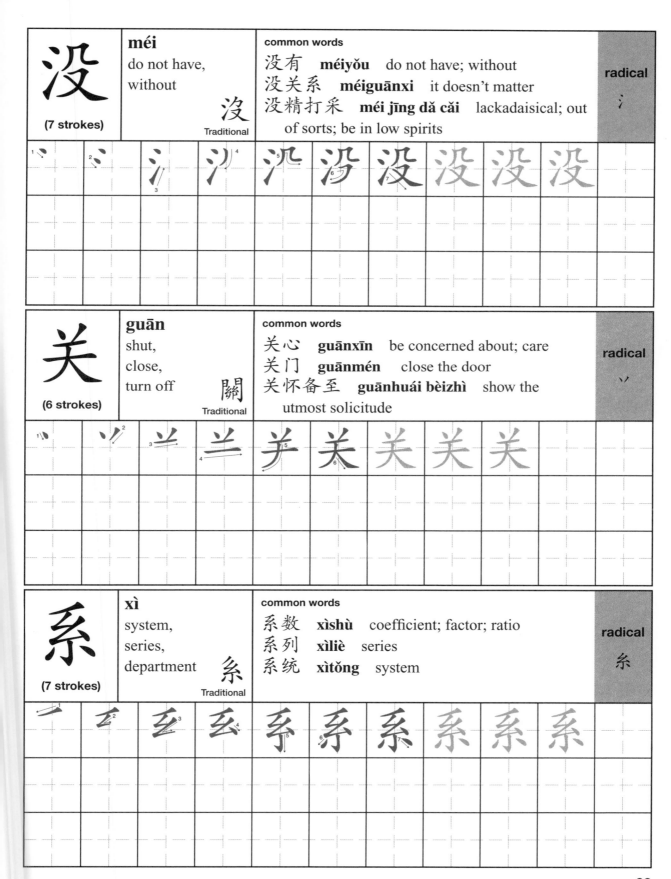

| 没 (7 strokes) | **méi** do not have, without | 没 Traditional | **common words** 没有 **méiyǒu** do not have; without 没关系 **méiguānxi** it doesn't matter 没精打采 **méi jīng dǎ cǎi** lackadaisical; out of sorts; be in low spirits | radical 氵 |

| 关 (6 strokes) | **guān** shut, close, turn off | 關 Traditional | **common words** 关心 **guānxīn** be concerned about; care 关门 **guānmén** close the door 关怀备至 **guānhuái bèizhì** show the utmost solicitude | radical 丷 |

| 系 (7 strokes) | **xì** system, series, department | 系 Traditional | **common words** 系数 **xìshù** coefficient; factor; ratio 系列 **xìliè** series 系统 **xìtǒng** system | radical 糸 |

再	**zài**	**common words**	radical
(6 strokes)	again, once more, further	再见　**zàijiàn**　good bye 再次　**zàicì**　once again; one more time 再接再厉　**zàijiē zàilì**　to make persistent efforts	一

一　丆　冂　冂　再　再　再　再　再

见	**jiàn**	**common words**	radical
(4 strokes)	see, meet with, view 見 **Traditional**	见面　**jiànmiàn**　meet; see 见解　**jiànjiě**　view; opinion 见多识广　**jiànduō shíguǎng**　experienced and knowledgeable	见

丨　冂　贝　见　见　见　见

WORD PRACTICE

谢谢 **xièxie** thank you, thanks

谢	谢								

不客气 **búkèqì** you are welcome

不	客	气						

对不起 **duìbùqǐ** sorry, excuse me

对	不	起						

没关系 **méiguānxi** it doesn't matter

没	关	系						

再见 **zàijiàn** good bye

再	见								

1. Draw a line from the pinyin to its matching Chinese character.

nǐ	zài	méi	xiè	kè	guān	qǐ	xì	jiàn	qì
谢	你	客	气	起	没	系	关	见	再

2. Rearrange the words to form correct sentences.

1) 好们你！

   _____

2) 谢谢，我好很！

   _____

3) 没关系，不气客！

   _____

4) 你们谢谢！

   _____

5) 我很兴们高。

   _____

3. Rewrite the words in Chinese characters.

thank you   (   )   you are welcome   (   )

sorry   (   )   it doesn't matter   (   )

4. Read the dialogue. Choose the correct words from the boxes to fill in the brackets.

很好	吗	不客气	再见	认识	呢

小明　：　你好（　　　　　）？

东东　：　我很好，你呢？

小明　：　我也（　　　　　　　　）。你叫什么名字？

东东　：　我叫东东，你（　　　　　）？

小明　：　我叫小明。很高兴（　　　　　　　）你。

东东　：　我也是，谢谢！

小明　：　（　　　　　　　），再见！

东东　：　（　　　　　　　）！

分	**fēn** divide, minutes (time)	**common words** 分数 **fēnshù** marks (score); fraction 分析 **fēnxī** analysis 分钟 **fēnzhōng** minutes (time)	**radical** 八
(4 strokes)			

ノ	八	分	分	分	分	分			

钟	**zhōng** clock, bell 鐘 Traditional	**common words** 钟情 **zhōngqíng** be deeply in love 钟表 **zhōngbiǎo** clocks and watches 钟灵毓秀 **zhōng líng yù xiù** (idiom) a favorable ambience nurtures talent	**radical** 钅
(9 strokes)			

ノ	𠂉	𠂊	乍	金	钅	钅	钊	钟	钟	钟
钟										

点	**diǎn** dot, o'clock, point 點 Traditional	**common words** 点名 **diǎnmíng** roll call; mention somebody by name 点菜 **diǎncài** to order dishes 点石成金 **diǎn shí chéng jīn** (idiom) touch a stone and turn it into gold	**radical** 灬
(9 strokes)			

丨	上	占	点	点	点	点	点	点	点	点
点										

昨	**zuó** yesterday	**common words**		radical 日
(9 strokes)		昨天　**zuótiān**　yesterday 昨日　**zuórì**　yesterday 昨晚　**zuówǎn**　last night		

丨	冂	月	日	昨	昨	昨	昨	昨	昨
昨									

今	**jīn** present	**common words**		radical 人
(4 strokes)		今天　**jīntiān**　today 今生　**jīnshēng**　this life 今非昔比　**jīn fēi xī bǐ**　the present cannot compare with the past		

丿	人	仐	今	今	今	今			

明	**míng** bright	**common words**		radical 日
(8 strokes)		明白　**míngbái**　understand 明天　**míngtiān**　tomorrow 明知故问　**míngzhī gù wèn**　ask while knowing the answer		

丨	冂	月	日	明	明	明	明	明	明	明

天 **tiān**
day,
sky

(4 strokes)

common words
天才　**tiāncái**　genius; talent
天气　**tiānqì**　weather
天长地久　**tiāncháng dì jiǔ**　enduring as the
universe; eternal

radical
一

上 **shàng**
above,
go up

(3 strokes)

common words
上班　**shàngbān**　go to work
上午　**shàngwǔ**　morning
上行下效　**shàngxíng xià xiào**　subordinates
follow the example of their superiors

radical
一

下 **xià**
below,
under,
next

(3 strokes)

common words
下班　**xiàbān**　get off work
下午　**xiàwǔ**　afternoon
下笔成章　**xiàbǐ chéngzhāng**　compose
something coherent without much effort

radical
一

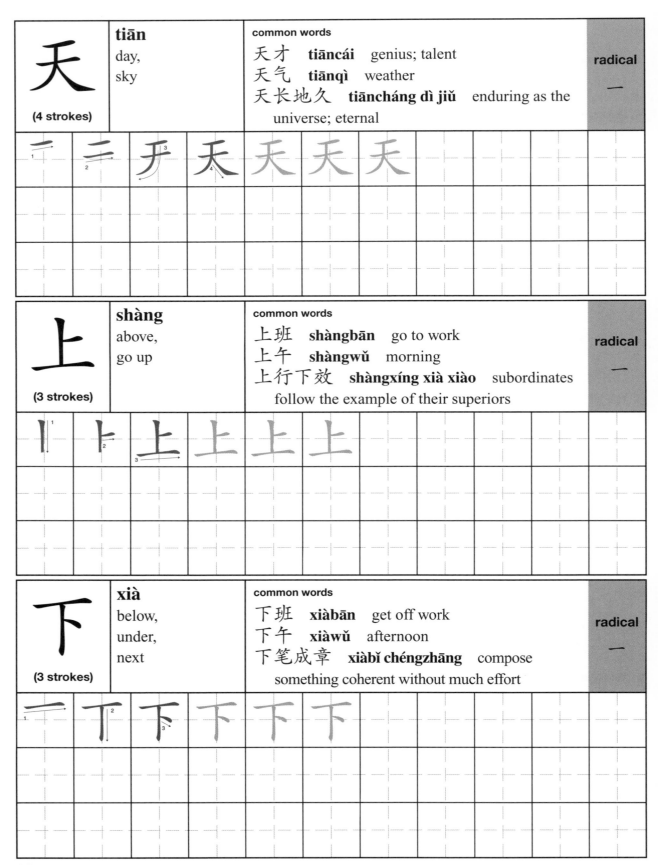

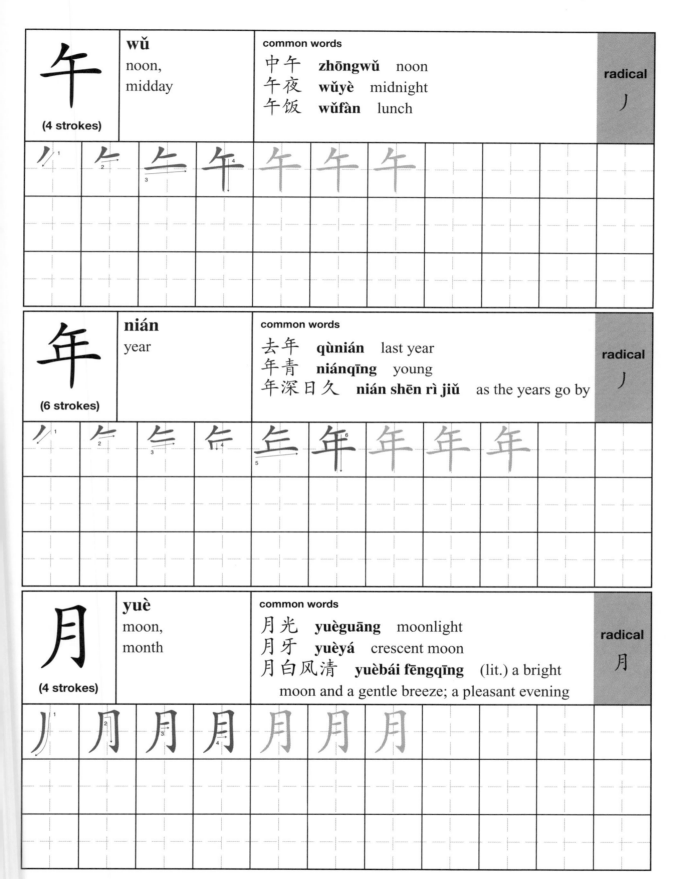

午	wǔ
	noon, midday
(4 strokes)	

common words

中午　**zhōngwǔ**　noon
午夜　**wǔyè**　midnight
午饭　**wǔfàn**　lunch

radical
丿

年	nián
	year
(6 strokes)	

common words

去年　**qùnián**　last year
年青　**niánqīng**　young
年深日久　**nián shēn rì jiǔ**　as the years go by

radical
丿

月	yuè
	moon, month
(4 strokes)	

common words

月光　**yuèguāng**　moonlight
月牙　**yuèyá**　crescent moon
月白风清　**yuèbái fēngqīng**　(lit.) a bright
moon and a gentle breeze; a pleasant evening

radical
月

日	**rì**	**common words**	
(4 strokes)	day	日出 **rìchū** sunrise 日夜 **rìyè** day and night 日新月异 **rìxīn yuè yì** change with each 　　　　passing day	**radical** 日

星	**xīng**	**common words**	
(9 strokes)	star	星河 **xīnghé** the milky way; galaxy 星光 **xīngguāng** starlight 星期 **xīngqī** week	**radical** 日

期	**qī**	**common words**	
(12 strokes)	period of time	期刊 **qīkān** periodical 期限 **qīxiàn** time limit; deadline 期期艾艾 **qīqī àiài** stammer; stutter	**radical** 月

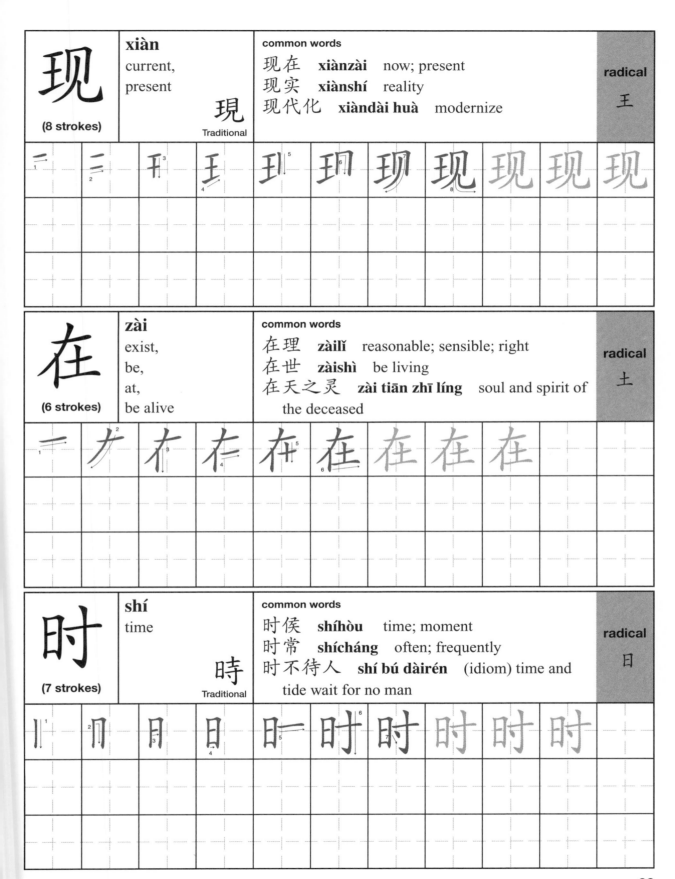

| 现 | **xiàn** current, present | **common words** | | radical 王 |
| (8 strokes) | 現 Traditional | 现在 **xiànzài** now; present
现实 **xiànshí** reality
现代化 **xiàndài huà** modernize | | |

| 在 | **zài** exist, be, at, be alive | **common words** | | radical 土 |
| (6 strokes) | | 在理 **zàilǐ** reasonable; sensible; right
在世 **zàishì** be living
在天之灵 **zài tiān zhī líng** soul and spirit of
the deceased | | |

| 时 | **shí** time | **common words** | | radical 日 |
| (7 strokes) | 時 Traditional | 时侯 **shíhòu** time; moment
时常 **shícháng** often; frequently
时不待人 **shí bú dàirén** (idiom) time and
tide wait for no man | | |

候	**hòu** wait, time	**common words** 候车　**hòuchē**　wait for a bus or train 候补　**hòubǔ**　reserve (candidate); substitute 候机室　**hòujīshì**　airport lounge or waiting room	**radical** 亻

(10 strokes)

亻	亻	亻	亻	伫	伫	伫	伫	伫	候	候
候	候									

WORD PRACTICE

分钟　**fēnzhōng**　minutes

分	钟								

昨天　**zuótiān**　yesterday

昨	天								

今天　**jīntiān**　today

今	天								

明天　**míngtiān**　tomorrow

明	天								

上午　**shàngwǔ**　morning

上	午								

中午　**zhōngwǔ**　noon

中	午									

下午　**xiàwǔ**　afternoon

下	午									

星期　**xīngqī**　week

星	期									

现在　**xiànzài**　now, present

现	在									

时候　**shíhòu**　time, moment

时	候									

去年　**qùnián**　last year

去	年									

天气　**tiānqì**　weather

天	气									

1. **Read the pinyin. Choose the correct characters to complete the sentence.**

   1) 明天是 _____ (xīngqī yī)。

      今天　　　星期三　　　现在　　　星期一

   2) 今天是 _____ (shī yī yuè wǔ hào)。

      八月九号　　　十一月五号　　　三月七号　　　四月十一号

   3) 昨天是 _____ (xīngqī liù)。

      七月三号　　　九月十号　　　星期六　　　星期天

   4) 今天是 _____ (xīngqī rì)。

      星期一　　　星期日　　　十月三号　　　一月四号

   5) 明天是 _____ (shí ér yuè qī hào)。

      十二月七号　　　二月七号　　　十二月九号　　　五月五号

2. **Fill in the blanks by choosing A, B, C or D. Each sentence can only be used once.**

   A. 明天是星期五吗？

   B. 今天是三月十号吗？

   C. 现在是下午三点二十四分。

   D. 是的，昨天是星期四。

   1) A: _____?
       B: 是的，明天是星期五。

2) A: _____?

    B: 不是，今天不是三月十号。

3) A: 昨天是星期四吗？

    B: _____?

4) A: 现在是几点几分？

    B: _____?

3. Look at each box. Fill in the correct characters to complete the sentence.

三月六号 星期五	昨天是三月六号, 星期五。 今天是( )月( )号, 星期( )。 明天是( )月( )号, 星期( )。
5月12号 星期二	今天是五月十二号, 星期二。 ( )是五月十三号, 星期( )。 昨天是( ), 星期( )。
九月九号 星期四	明天是九月九号, 星期四。 今天是( )月( )号, ( )。 昨天是( )月( )号, ( )。

4. Write the corresponding time in Chinese characters.

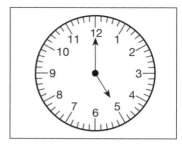 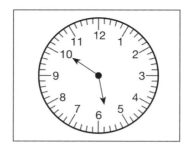 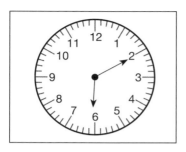

_____   _____   _____

5. Rewrite the sentences in Chinese characters.

1) What day is today? Today is Monday.

_____

2) What day was yesterday? Yesterday was Sunday.

_____

3) What day is tomorrow? Tomorrow is Tuesday.

_____

4) Is today July fifteenth? Yes, today is July fifteenth.

_____

5) Was yesterday August sixth? No, yesterday was August seventh.

_____

6) Will tomorrow be December first? Yes, tomorrow will be December first.

_____

7) What time is it now? It is six thirty.

_____

8) Is it ten after twelve? No, isn't. It's five after.

_____

9) It is eleven twenty in the morning.

_____

10) Isn't it three in the afternoon? Yes, it is three in the afternoon.

_____

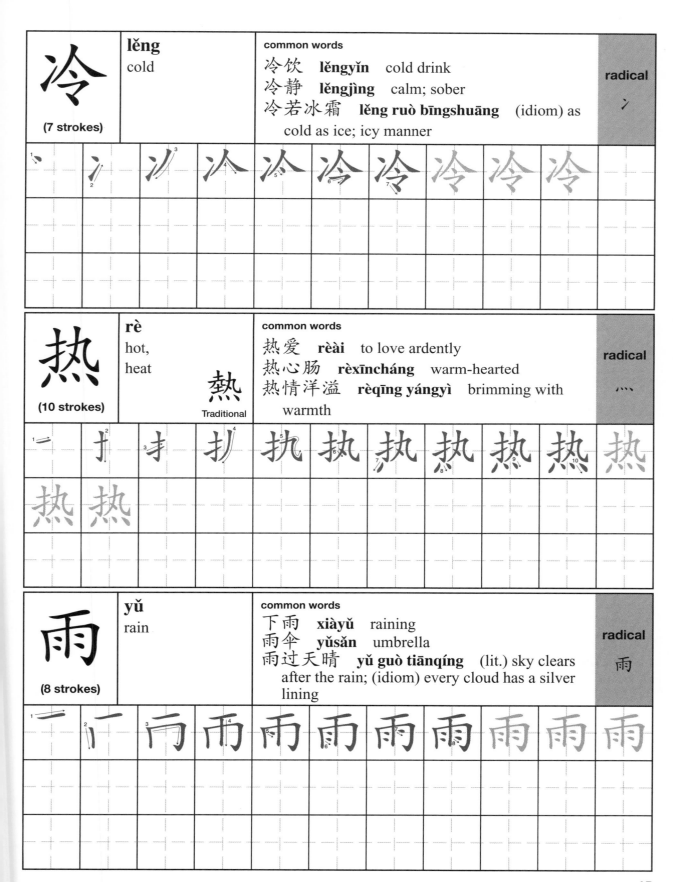

| 冷 (7 strokes) | **lěng** cold | **common words** 冷饮　**lěngyǐn**　cold drink 冷静　**lěngjìng**　calm; sober 冷若冰霜　**lěng ruò bīngshuāng**　(idiom) as cold as ice; icy manner | radical 冫 |

| 热 (10 strokes) | **rè** hot, heat 熱 Traditional | **common words** 热爱　**rèài**　to love ardently 热心肠　**rèxīncháng**　warm-hearted 热情洋溢　**rèqīng yángyì**　brimming with warmth | radical 灬 |

| 雨 (8 strokes) | **yǔ** rain | **common words** 下雨　**xiàyǔ**　raining 雨伞　**yǔsǎn**　umbrella 雨过天晴　**yǔ guò tiānqíng**　(lit.) sky clears after the rain; (idiom) every cloud has a silver lining | radical 雨 |

45

了	**le/liǎo**	**common words**	**radical**
(2 strokes)	a particle	吃了　**chīle**　have eaten 别说了　**biéshuōle**　don't talk about it any more 了不起　**liǎobùqǐ**　amazing; terrific	一

了 了 了 了 了

看	**kàn**	**common words**	**radical**
(9 strokes)	see, watch	看见　**kànjiàn**　to see 看法　**kànfǎ**　view; opinion 看风使舵　**kànfēng shǐduò**　adapt oneself to circumstances	目

一 二 三 尹 手 看 看 看 看 看 看

看

怎	**zěn**	**common words**	**radical**
(9 strokes)	how, why	怎么样　**zěnmeyàng**　how?; how are things? 不怎么　**bùzěnme**　not very; not much 怎么得了　**zěnme déliǎo**　What a terrible thing it would be!	心

丿 乍 乍 乍 乍 乍 怎 怎 怎 怎 怎

怎

样	yàng appearance, shape	**common words**		radical
(10 strokes)	樣 Traditional	样式　**yàngshì**　style; form; pattern 样子　**yàngzi**　appearance; manner 样本　**yàngběn**　sample; specimen		木

一	十	才	木	术	术	栏	栏	栏	样	样

样	样									

WORD PRACTICE

下雨　**xiàyǔ**　raining

下	雨						

怎么样　**zěnmeyàng**　how? how are things?

怎	么	样					

看见　**kànjiàn**　to see

看	见						

1. Circle the correct pinyin for the underlined character.

<u>今</u>（ jīn jīng ）天   <u>天</u>（ tiān tān ）气

<u>明</u>（ míng mín ）天   <u>下</u>（ xiè xià ）雨

<u>什</u>（ shén shéng ）么   <u>很</u>（ něng lěng ）<u>冷</u>

<u>几</u>（ qǐ jǐ ）点   <u>怎</u>（ zěn zěng ）么

<u>客</u>（ kè gè ）气   <u>关</u>（ qì xì ）<u>系</u>

2. Choose correct words from the box to complete each sentence.

天气	热	雨	刮风	看见

1) 今天 ＿＿＿＿＿＿＿＿＿＿ 怎么样？

2) 明天会下 ＿＿＿＿＿＿＿＿＿＿ 吗？

3) 昨天天气很 ＿＿＿＿＿＿＿＿＿＿ 。

4) 我星期三 ＿＿＿＿＿＿＿＿＿＿ 了她。

5) 星期天会 ＿＿＿＿＿＿＿＿＿＿ 吗？

3. Form new words by joining characters in box 1 with the characters in box 2. Some words can be used more than once.

1)

天	今	很	怎	刮	昨	下	明

2)

冷	风	热	么	雨	天	气

4. Make your own sentences using the characters provided.

Example: 怎么样： 今天天气怎么样？

1) 看见： _____

2) 天气： _____

3) 下雨： _____

5. Rearrange the characters to form correct sentences.

1) 下午今天会吗刮风？ _____

2) 下雨会上午星期五。 _____

3) 很热天气今天。 _____

4) 下午明天怎么样天气？ _____

5) 上午昨天很冷。 _____

6) 不热今天下午。 _____

7) 明天刮大风不会。 _____

8) 下雨看见吗了你？ _____

6. Read and copy these Chinese phrases into the brackets.

下雨了！（　　　　　）　刮风了！（　　　　　）

看见了！（　　　　　）　怎么了？（　　　　　）

谢谢了！（　　　　　）　再见了！（　　　　　）

7. Rewrite the paragraph in Chinese characters.

Today is Sunday. It is now seven o'clock in the morning. How is the weather today? Today's weather is not good, it is so cold! There is heavy wind and it is raining.

_____

_____

_____

8. Rewrite these sentences in English.

昨天是星期六。昨天天气怎么样？昨天很热。

_____

今天天气怎么样？今天很冷，会刮风会下雨，今天天气很不好。

_____

_____

明天天气怎么样？明天天气会很好，不冷也不热，没有大风也没有雨。

_____

_____

学	xué	common words	radical
(8 strokes)	to study, to learn 學 Traditional	学校 **xuéxiào** school 学习 **xuéxí** study; learn 学生 **xuésheng** student	子

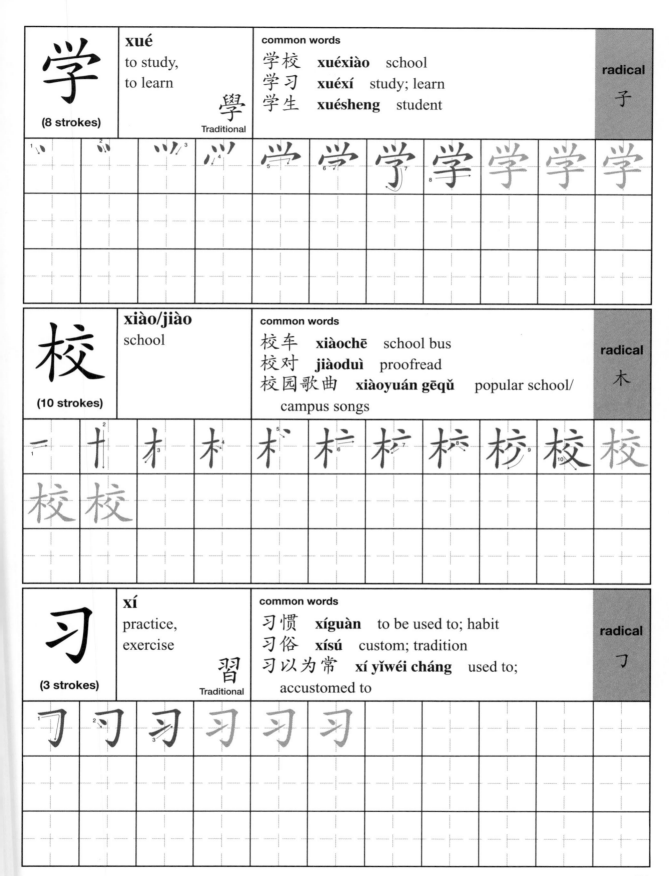

校	xiào/jiào	common words	radical
(10 strokes)	school	校车 **xiàochē** school bus 校对 **jiàoduì** proofread 校园歌曲 **xiàoyuán gēqǔ** popular school/ campus songs	木

习	xí	common words	radical
(3 strokes)	practice, exercise 習 Traditional	习惯 **xíguàn** to be used to; habit 习俗 **xísú** custom; tradition 习以为常 **xí yǐwéi cháng** used to; accustomed to	习

| 老 (6 strokes) | **lǎo** old | **common words** 老人 **lǎorén** the elderly
老师 **lǎoshī** teacher
老马识途 **lǎomǎ shítú** (idiom) an old horse
knows the way; an old hand knows the ropes | radical 老 |

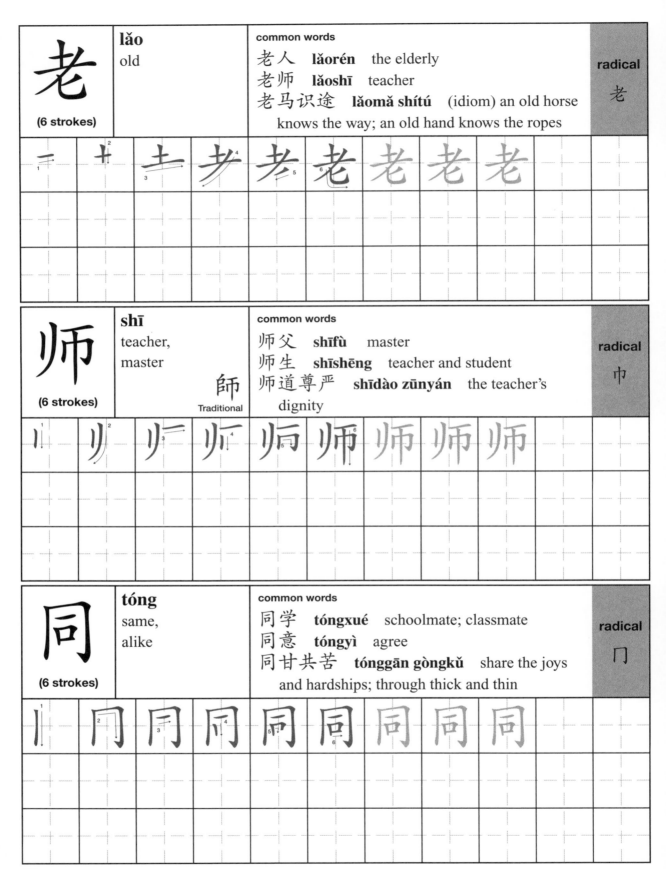

| 师 (6 strokes) | **shī** teacher, master

師 **Traditional** | **common words** 师父 **shīfù** master
师生 **shīshēng** teacher and student
师道尊严 **shīdào zūnyán** the teacher's
dignity | radical 巾 |

| 同 (6 strokes) | **tóng** same, alike | **common words** 同学 **tóngxué** schoolmate; classmate
同意 **tóngyì** agree
同甘共苦 **tónggān gòngkǔ** share the joys
and hardships; through thick and thin | radical 冂 |

做	zuò	common words	radical
(11 strokes)	do, make, produce	做客　**zuòkè**　be a guest 做饭　**zuòfàn**　prepare a meal; to cook 做贼心虚　**zuòzéi xīnxū**　(idiom) as guilty as 　　a thief; guilty conscience	亻

丿　亻　仁　什　什　估　估　做　做　做　做

做　做　做

听	tīng	common words	radical
(7 strokes)	listen, hear 聽 **Traditional**	听力　**tīnglì**　hearing/listening ability 听说　**tīngshuō**　be told; hearsay 听天由命　**tīngtiān yóumìng**　to submit to the 　　will of heaven	口

丨　口　口　吁　听　听　听　听　听　听

说	shuō	common words	radical
(9 strokes)	speak, talk 説 **Traditional**	说话　**shuōhuà**　speak; talk 说书　**shuōshū**　storytelling 说一不二　**shuō yī bú èr**　mean what one says; 　　to keep one's word	讠

丶　讠　讠　讠　说　说　说　说　说　说

说

读	dú read		common words		radical 讠

读音 **dúyīn** pronunciation
读者 **dúzhě** reader
读书破万卷 **dúshū pò wànjuàn** (lit.) have read more than ten thousand scrolls; well read

读 (10 strokes) | **讀 Traditional**

丶	讠	订	讧	诗	诗	诗	读	读	读
读	读								

写	xiě write, compose		common words		radical 冖

写信 **xiěxìn** to write a letter
写生 **xiěshēng** to sketch from nature
写字楼 **xiězìlóu** office building

写 (5 strokes) | **寫 Traditional**

冖	冖	写	写	写	写	写			

打	dǎ hit, beat		common words		radical 扌

打工 **dǎgōng** to do a casual work
打开 **dǎkāi** to open
打电话 **dǎdiànhuà** to make a phone call

打 (5 strokes)

一	扌	扌	打	打	打	打	打		

书	**shū** book, to write, document 書 *Traditional*	**common words** 书法　**shūfǎ**　calligraphy 书店　**shūdiàn**　bookstore 书香门第　**shūxiāng méndì**　literary family	radical 丨
(4 strokes)			

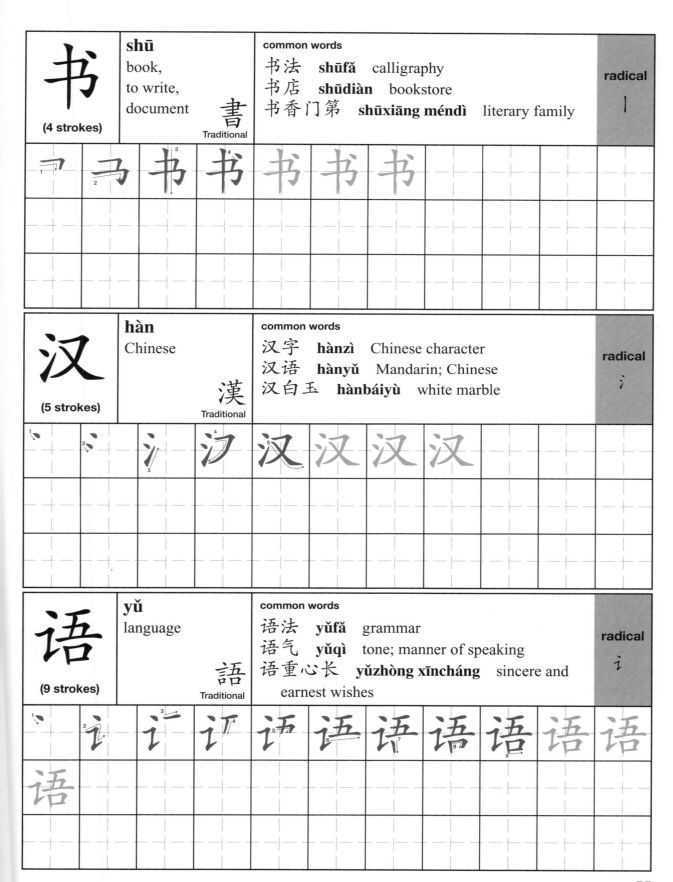

汉	**hàn** Chinese 漢 *Traditional*	**common words** 汉字　**hànzì**　Chinese character 汉语　**hànyǔ**　Mandarin; Chinese 汉白玉　**hànbáiyù**　white marble	radical 氵
(5 strokes)			

语	**yǔ** language 語 *Traditional*	**common words** 语法　**yǔfǎ**　grammar 语气　**yǔqì**　tone; manner of speaking 语重心长　**yǔzhòng xīncháng**　sincere and earnest wishes	radical 讠
(9 strokes)			

电	diàn	common words	radical
(5 strokes)	electricity, electronic 電 Traditional	电传　**diànchuán**　telex 电话　**diànhuà**　telephone 电子邮件　**diànzǐ yóujiàn**　email	丨

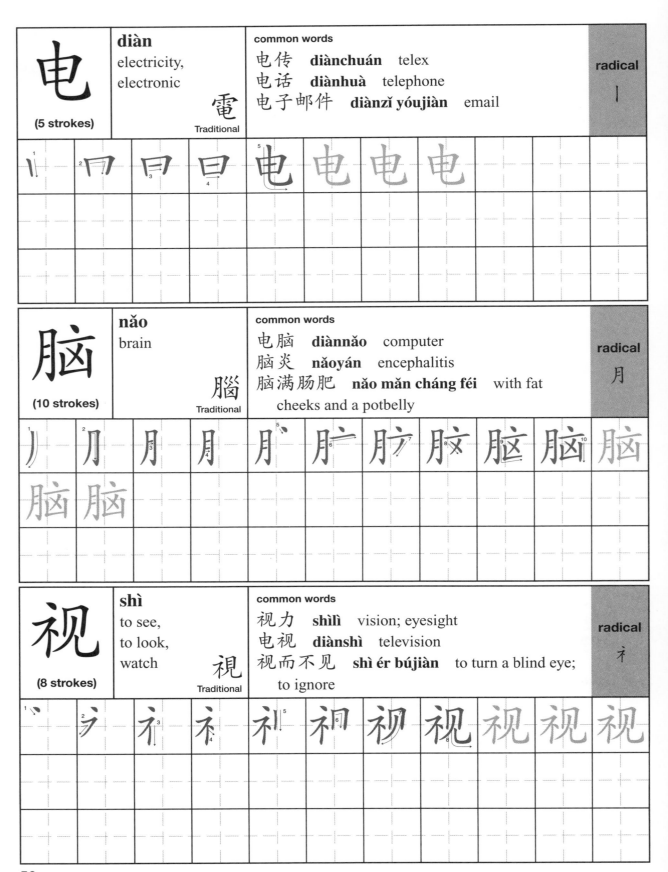

脑	nǎo	common words	radical
(10 strokes)	brain 腦 Traditional	电脑　**diànnǎo**　computer 脑炎　**nǎoyán**　encephalitis 脑满肠肥　**nǎo mǎn cháng féi**　with fat cheeks and a potbelly	月

视	shì	common words	radical
(8 strokes)	to see, to look, watch 視 Traditional	视力　**shìlì**　vision; eyesight 电视　**diànshì**　television 视而不见　**shì ér bújiàn**　to turn a blind eye; 　to ignore	衤

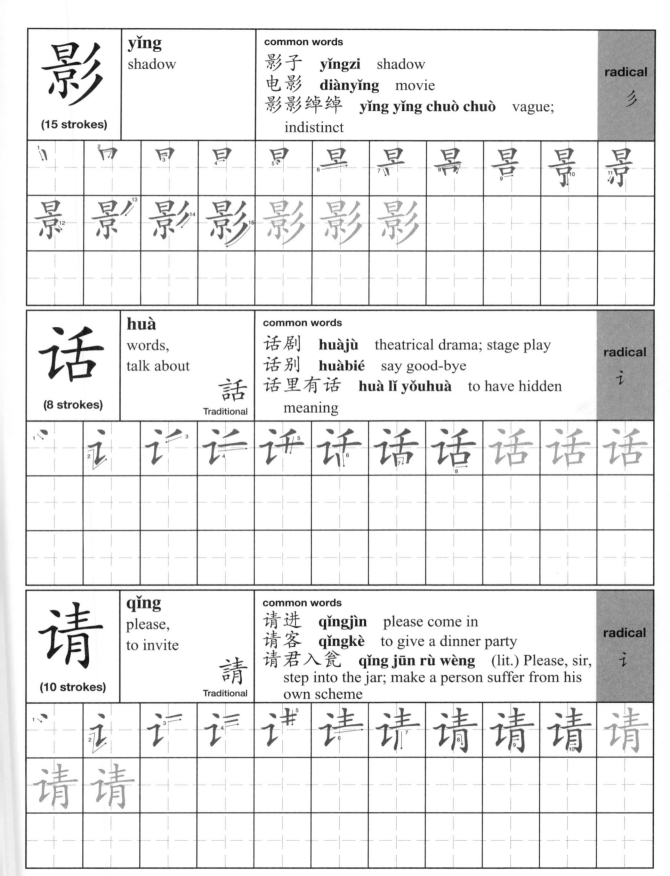

影 yǐng — shadow

(15 strokes)

radical 彡

common words

影子　**yǐngzi**　shadow
电影　**diànyǐng**　movie
影影绰绰　**yǐng yǐng chuò chuò**　vague; indistinct

话 huà — words, talk about

話 Traditional

(8 strokes)

radical 讠

common words

话剧　**huàjù**　theatrical drama; stage play
话别　**huàbié**　say good-bye
话里有话　**huà lǐ yǒuhuà**　to have hidden meaning

请 qǐng — please, to invite

請 Traditional

(10 strokes)

radical 讠

common words

请进　**qǐngjìn**　please come in
请客　**qǐngkè**　to give a dinner party
请君入瓮　**qǐng jūn rù wèng**　(lit.) Please, sir, step into the jar; make a person suffer from his own scheme

WORD PRACTICE

学校 **xuéxiào** school

学	校								

学习 **xuéxí** study, learn

学	习								

老师 **lǎoshī** teacher

老	师								

学生 **xuésheng** student

学	生								

同学 **tóngxué** schoolmate, classmate

同	学								

汉语 **hànyǔ** Mandarin, Chinese

汉	语								

汉字 **hànzì** Mandarin, Chinese character

汉	字								

电脑 **diànnǎo** computer

电	脑								

电视 **diànshì** television

电	视								

电影 **diànyǐng** movie

电	影								

影子 **yǐngzi** shadow

影	子								

打电话 **dǎdiànhuà** to make a phone call

打	电	话							

说话 **shuōhuà** to talk, speak

说	话								

书店 **shūdiàn** bookstore

书	店								

脑子 **nǎozi** brain

脑	子								

1. **Read and copy these Chinese phrases into the brackets.**

请听 (   )   请说   (   )

请读 (   )   请写   (   )

请看 (   )   请打字 (   )

2. **Identify the characters with the same radicals. Write them in the space provided.**

你	认	听	们	话	样
叫	什	谢	说	做	呢
校	读	他	吗	请	识

亻 ___   ___   ___   ___   ___

讠 ___   ___   ___   ___   ___   ___

木 ___   ___

口 ___   ___   ___

3. Answer the questions in Chinese characters (pinyin given in brackets).

1) A: 你在看什么？ B: 我在 _____ (kànshū)。

A: 你同学在看什么？ B: 我同学在 _____ (kàn diànshì)。

2) A: 你在写什么？ B: 我在 _____ (xiězì)。

A: 老师在写什么？ B: 老师在 _____ (xiěshū)。

3) A: 他在做什么？ B: 他在 _____ (xué hànyǔ)。

A: 她在做什么？ B: 她在 _____ (dǎdiànhuà)。

4. Make your own sentences using the characters provided.

Example: 学 ： 我姐姐在学汉语。

1) 看 : _____

2) 读 : _____

3) 写字 : _____

4) 说汉语 : _____

5) 做什么 : _____

5. Substitute the underline characters to form new sentences.

Example: 他是我的老师。

她，同学 她是我的同学。

我天天去上学。

你，看书 _____

老师，去学校 _____

学生，读书 _____

我，学汉语 _____

她，写汉字 _____

他们在打电话。

我们，看电影 _____

学生们，学习 _____

我同学，看电视 _____

老师们，学校 _____

他们，看书 _____

6. Answer the questions. Write your answers in Chinese characters.

1) 你们学校有多少老师和学生？

   _____

2) 你在学校学习汉语吗？

   _____

3) 你的汉语怎么样？

   _____

4) 你天天写汉字吗？

   _____

家	**jiā** home, family	**common words** 家庭 **jiātíng** family 家产 **jiāchǎn** family property 家喻户晓 **jiā yù hù xiǎo** well known; a household name	radical 宀
(10 strokes)			

宀	宀	宀	宇	宇	宁	家	家	家	家	家
家	家									

爸	**bà** father	**common words** 爸爸 **bàba** dad; father 老爸 **lǎobà** old dad; father 爸妈 **bàmā** father and mother	radical 父
(8 strokes)			

丷	八	少	父	爷	爷	釜	爸	爸	爸	爸

妈	**mā** mother 媽 Traditional	**common words** 妈妈 **māma** mother; mum 姑妈 **gūmā** aunt (from father's family) 姨妈 **yímā** aunt (from mother's family)	radical 女
(6 strokes)			

乚	女	女	妈	妈	妈	妈	妈			

女	nǚ female	**common words**	radical 女
(3 strokes)		女士 **nǚshì** madam; lady 女儿 **nǚér** daughter 女扮男装 **nǚ bàn nánzhuāng** a woman 　　disguised as a man	

人	女	女	女	女	女				

儿	ér child, a suffix	**common words**	radical 儿
(2 strokes)	兒 Traditional	儿歌 **érgē** children's song; nursery rhyme 儿戏 **érxì** child play; a trifling matter 儿子 **érzi** son	

丿	儿	儿	儿	儿					

子	zǐ son, child, seed	**common words**	radical 子
(3 strokes)		子女 **zǐnǚ** sons and daughters; children 子弟 **zǐdì** sons and younger brothers; children 子孙满堂 **zǐsūn mǎntáng** be blessed 　　with many children and grandchildren	

了	了	子	子	子	子				

65

先	**xiān** earlier, before, prior	**common words** 先生 **xiānsheng** mister; husband 先兆 **xiānzhào** omen; portent 先见之明 **xiānjiàn zhī míng** prophetic vision; foresight	radical 儿

(6 strokes)

ノ	⌐	牛	生	歩	先	先	先	先	

生	**shēng** to be born, raw	**common words** 生命 **shēngmìng** life 生存 **shēngcún** subsist; exist 生气勃勃 **shēngqì bóbó** full of vitality; full of life	radical 丿

(5 strokes)

ノ	⌐	乍	牛	生	生	生	生		

姐	**jiě** older sister	**common words** 姐弟 **jiědì** older sister and younger brother 姐夫 **jiěfu** older brother-in-law 小姐 **xiǎojiě** miss; young lady	radical 女

(8 strokes)

㇄	女	女	奶	姐	姐	姐	姐	姐	姐	姐

这	**zhè**	common words	
	this	这里 **zhèlǐ** here	**radical**
		这些 **zhèxiē** these	
(7 strokes)	這 Traditional	这儿 **zhèr** here	辶

那	**nà**	common words	
	that	那里 **nàlǐ** there	**radical**
		那些 **nàxiē** those	
(6 strokes)		那儿 **nàr** there	阝

是	**shì**	common words	
	yes,	是否 **shìfǒu** whether or not; if	**radical**
	to be	是味儿 **shìwèier** have the right taste	
		是非曲直 **shìfēi qūzhí** right and wrong;	日
(9 strokes)		truth and falsehood; pros and cons	

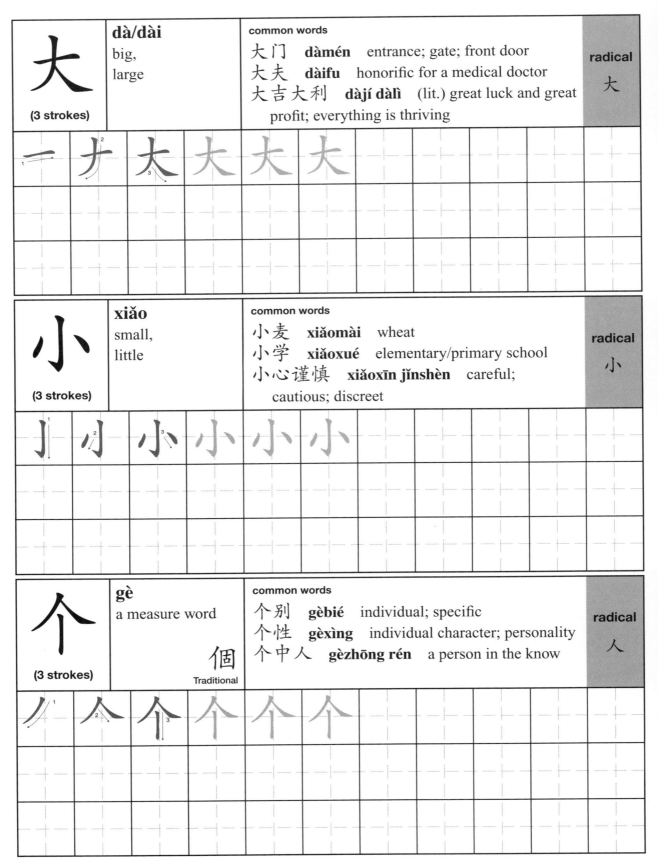

大 dà/dài

big, large

(3 strokes)

radical 大

common words

大门 **dàmén** entrance; gate; front door
大夫 **dàifu** honorific for a medical doctor
大吉大利 **dàjí dàlì** (lit.) great luck and great profit; everything is thriving

小 xiǎo

small, little

(3 strokes)

radical 小

common words

小麦 **xiǎomài** wheat
小学 **xiǎoxué** elementary/primary school
小心谨慎 **xiǎoxīn jǐnshèn** careful; cautious; discreet

个 gè

a measure word

個 Traditional

(3 strokes)

radical 人

common words

个别 **gèbié** individual; specific
个性 **gèxìng** individual character; personality
个中人 **gèzhōng rén** a person in the know

人	rén	common words	
	person, people	人工 **réngōng** artificial; manual work	radical
(2 strokes)		人类 **rénlèi** humanity; mankind; human race	人
		人杰地灵 **rénjié dìlíng** (idiom) the greatness of man lends glory to a place; illustrious hero	

丿 人 人 人 人

几	jǐ	common words	
	several, a few, almost	几个 **jǐgè** a few	radical
(2 strokes)	幾 Traditional	几时 **jǐshí** what time; when	几
		几起几落 **jǐqǐ jǐluò** several ups and downs	

几 几 几 几 几

岁	suì	common words	
	year, classifier for years (of age)	岁月 **suìyuè** years; time	radical
(6 strokes)	歲 Traditional	岁数 **suìshu** age (years old)	山
		岁寒三友 **suìhán sānyǒu** (lit.) three durable plants of winter—pine, bamboo and plum blossom; three 'cold-weather' friends	

丨 山 山 岁 岁 岁 岁 岁 岁

有

yǒu
have,
has

(6 strokes)

common words

有名　**yǒumíng**　well known; famous

有机　**yǒujī**　organic

有教无类　**yǒu jiào wú lèi**　education for
everyone, irrespective of background

radical
月

谁

shéi/shuí
who

誰
Traditional

(10 strokes)

common words

谁知　**shuízhī**　(lit.) who knows; unexpectedly

谁的　**shuíde**　whose

谁解其味　**shuíjiě qíwèi**　who can explain
the real taste

radical
讠

和

hé
and,
harmony,
sum

(8 strokes)

common words

和平　**hépíng**　peace

和气　**héqì**　friendly; polite

和风细雨　**héfēng xìyǔ**　(lit.) gentle breeze
and fine drizzle; in a gentle and mild way

radical
禾

| 住 (7 strokes) | **zhù** live, stay | **common words** 住户　**zhùhù**　household; resident 住址　**zhùzhǐ**　address 住宅区　**zhùzháiqū**　residential area | **radical** 亻 |

| 丿 | 亻 | 彳 | 仁 | 仨 | 住 | 住 | 住 | 住 | 住 |

| 的 (8 strokes) | **de/dí** a particle | **common words** 我的书　**wǒdeshū**　my book 红的花　**hóngdehuā**　red flower 的确　**díquè**　indeed; certainly; really | **radical** 白 |

| 丿 | 亻 | 白 | 自 | 白 | 白 | 的 | 的 | 的 | 的 | 的 |

WORD PRACTICE

爸爸 **bàba** father, dad

爸	爸								

妈妈 **māma** mother, mom

妈	妈								

儿子 **érzi** son

儿	子								

女儿 **nǚér** daughter

女	儿								

先生 **xiānsheng** mister, husband

先	生								

小姐 **xiǎojiě** miss, young lady

小	姐								

这儿 **zhèr** here

这	儿								

那儿 **nàr** there

那	儿								

1. Match the English with the pinyin and Chinese characters.

English	Pinyin	Chinese characters
father	**ěrzi**	爸爸
older sister	**xuéshēng**	妈妈
son	**xiānsheng**	医生
mother	**jiějie**	女儿
daughter	**māma**	姐姐
husband	**bàba**	老师
doctor	**xiǎojiě**	儿子
teacher	**nǚér**	学生
miss	**yīshēng**	先生
student	**lǎoshī**	小姐

2. Answer the questions using Chinese characters.

1) 这是谁？

    这是 _____ (my father)。

    这是谁？

    这是_____ (my mother)。

    这是谁？

    这是_____ (my older sister)。

2) 那是谁的家？

    那是_____ (my home)。

    那是谁的家？

    那是_____ (my daughter's home)。

    那是谁的家？

    那是_____ (my son's home)。

3) 你家有几个人？

    我家_____ (have four people)。

    他家有几个人？

    他家_____ (have two people)。

    她家有几个人？

    她家_____ (have three people)。

4) 你多大？

    我_____ (seventeen years old)。

    你的姐姐多大？

    我的姐姐_____ (twenty one years old)。

    你的同学呢？

    我的同学_____ (eighteen years old)。

3. Make your own sentences using the characters provided.

Example: 是不是 ：那是不是小明的书？

1) 是 ： _____

2) 不是 ： _____

3) 这是 ： _____

4) 那是 ： _____

5) 有 ： _____

6) 没有 ： _____

4. Use these characters to form phrases. Write them in the space provided.

妈	女	爸	先	这	那
姐	小	是	儿	学	怎
天	妈	我	爸	生	么
气	下	雨	家	子	样

1) <u>妈　妈</u>　　　　2) _____　　　　3) _____

4) _____　　　　5) _____　　　　6) _____

7) _____　　　　8) _____　　　　9) _____

10) _____　　　11) _____　　　12) _____

13) _____

5. Fill in the space with the appropriate words.

星期天	家	有	在下雨	看书
打	大学生	老师	学汉语	小学生

我家（　　　　　）四个人，爸爸，妈妈，姐姐和我。今

天是（　　　　　）。天气很冷，（　　　　　），我们都在

（　　　　　）里。我的爸爸和妈妈都是（　　　　　）。姐姐是

（　　　　　），我是（　　　　　）。现在，我的爸爸和妈妈在

（　　　　　），姐姐在（　　　　　），我在（　　　　　）电话。

| 喂 (12 strokes) | **wèi** hello, hey, to feed | **common words** 喂奶　**wèinǎi**　to breast-feed 喂养　**wèiyǎng**　feed; raise 喂婴儿　**wèiyīngér**　feeding a baby | **radical** 口 |

丨	口	口	叫	吲	喂	哽	喂	喂	喂	喂	喂
喂	喂	喂	喂								

| 朋 (8 strokes) | **péng** friend | **common words** 朋友　**péngyou**　friends 良朋　**liángpéng**　good friend; good companion 亲朋好友　**qīnpéng hǎoyǒu**　friends and family; kith and kin | **radical** 月 |

丿	月	月	月	朋	朋	朋	朋	朋	朋	朋

| 友 (4 strokes) | **yǒu** friend | **common words** 友人　**yǒurén**　friend 友情　**yǒuqíng**　friendship 友好城市　**yǒuhǎo chéngshì**　sister cities; twin cities | **radical** 又 |

一	𠂇	方	友	友	友	友	

77

| 哪 | **nǎ** which, what, how (9 strokes) | **common words** 哪个 **nǎgè** which 哪样 **nǎyàng** what kind; which kind 哪儿 **nǎr** where? | **radical** 口 |

| 前 | **qián** front, ahead, forward (9 strokes) | **common words** 前门 **qiánmén** front door 前面 **qiánmiàn** front 前所未有 **qián suǒ wèiyǒu** unprecedented; never previously existed | **radical** 刂 |

| 后 | **hòu** behind, back, later 後 Traditional (6 strokes) | **common words** 后天 **hòutiān** day after tomorrow 后面 **hòumiàn** back; behind 后会有期 **hòuhuì yǒuqī** we'll meet again some day | **radical** 口 |

里	lǐ inside, in, within	**common words**		radical
		里面 **lǐmiàn** inside		里
	裡	里屋 **lǐwū** inner room		
(7 strokes)	Traditional	里里外外 **lǐ lǐwài wài** inside and outside		

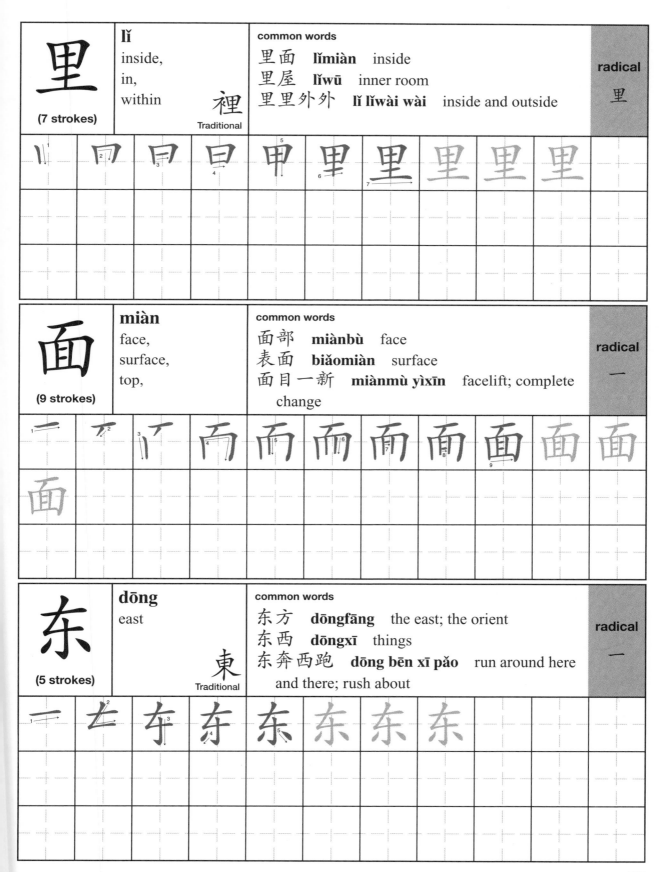

面	miàn face, surface, top,	**common words**		radical
		面部 **miànbù** face		一
		表面 **biǎomiàn** surface		
(9 strokes)		面目一新 **miànmù yìxīn** facelift; complete change		

东	dōng east	**common words**		radical
		东方 **dōngfāng** the east; the orient		一
	東	东西 **dōngxī** things		
(5 strokes)	Traditional	东奔西跑 **dōng bēn xī pǎo** run around here and there; rush about		

| 西
(6 strokes) | **xī**
west | **common words**
西方　**xīfāng**　the west
西式　**xīshì**　western style
西游记　**xī yóujì**　a famous Chinese novel—
　　　　　　　　Journey to the West (Monkey King) | **radical**
西 |

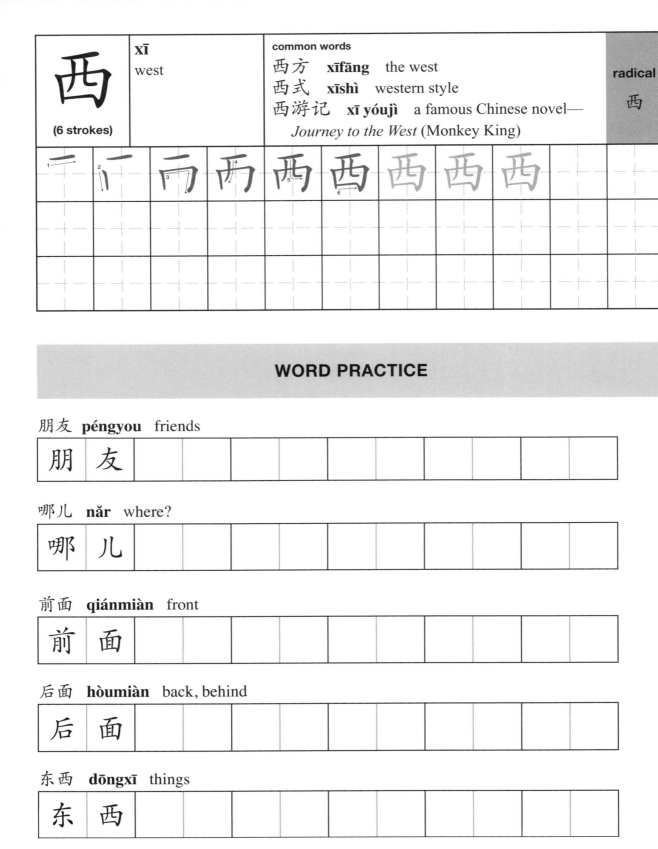

WORD PRACTICE

朋友 **péngyou**　friends

朋	友						

哪儿 **nǎr**　where?

哪	儿						

前面 **qiánmiàn**　front

前	面						

后面 **hòumiàn**　back, behind

后	面						

东西 **dōngxī**　things

东	西						

1. **Write the pinyin in the brackets.**

where ___ 哪儿　（　　　　），哪里　（　　　　）

here ___ 这儿　（　　　　），这里　（　　　　）

there ___ 那儿　（　　　　），那里　（　　　　）

front ___ 前　（　　　），前面　（　　　　）

back ___ 后　（　　　），后面　（　　　　）

inside ___ 里　（　　　），里面　（　　　　）

2. **Make your own sentences using the characters provided.**

Example: 在哪儿：你的学校在哪儿？

1) 在哪里：_____

2) 在那里：_____

3) 在前面：_____

4) 在后面：_____

5) 在里面：_____

6) 在东面：_____

7) 在西面：_____

8) 哪个人：_____

3. Read the dialog. Answer the questions in Chinese characters.

小明：喂，小明，你好！

东东：你好，小东！

小明：你在哪儿呢？

东东：我在我家里。

小明：你爸爸妈妈在家吗？

东东：他们不在家。

小明：你在家做什么？

东东：我在家看书。你呢，你在哪儿呢？

小明：我也在家。今天是星期六，我们去看电影，好吗？

东东：好啊！电影是几点钟？

小明：电影是下午四点钟。

东东：好，我们下午去看电影，再见！

小明：再见！

1) 今天是星期几？

   _____

2) 东东在哪儿？

   _____

3) 东东在家做什么？

   _____

4)　　小明和东东要去做什么？

　　　_____

5)　　电影是几点钟？

　　　_____

4. Connect the characters with the same radicals.

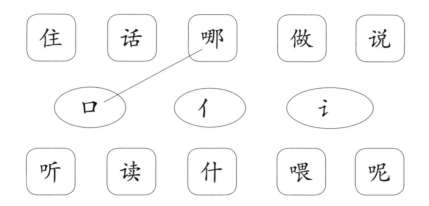

5. Substitute the underline characters to form a new sentence.

<u>你</u>在<u>哪儿</u>？

1)　<u>爸爸</u>，<u>学校</u>　　_____。

2)　<u>妈妈</u>，<u>家里</u>　　_____。

3)　<u>姐姐</u>，<u>那儿</u>　　_____。

4)　<u>我</u>，<u>这儿</u>　　_____。

5)　<u>你朋友</u>，<u>那里</u>　　_____。

书在哪里？

1) 电话，家里 _____。

2) 电脑，这里 _____。

3) 书，电脑前面 _____。

4) 电视，那里 _____。

5) 那个东西，电视后面 _____。

6. Rewrite the sentences in Chinese characters.

1) Where is your friend? She is in school.

_____

2) Who is that person? He is my classmate.

_____

3) Where do you live? My home is at the back of my school.

_____

4) Where is your older sister? She is there.

_____

医	**yī** cure, treat	**common words**	radical
(7 strokes)	醫 Traditional	医院　**yīyuàn**　hospital 医生　**yīshēng**　doctor 医术　**yīshù**　medical expertise; art of healing	匚

院	**yuàn** courtyard, institution	**common words**	radical
(9 strokes)		院子　**yuànzi**　courtyard; yard 院校　**yuànxiào**　university; college; academy 院士　**yuànshì**　academician; scholar	阝

工	**gōng** work, labor	**common words**	radical
(3 strokes)		工人　**gōngrén**　worker 工业　**gōngyè**　industry 工作　**gōngzuò**　work; job	工

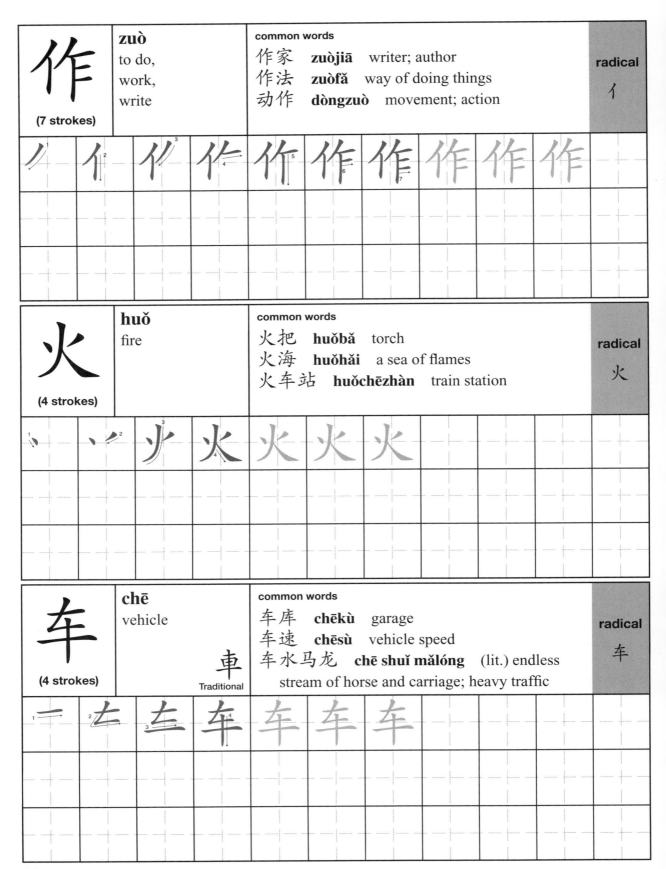

| 作 | **zuò** to do, work, write (7 strokes) | **common words** 作家 **zuòjiā** writer; author 作法 **zuòfǎ** way of doing things 动作 **dòngzuò** movement; action | **radical** 亻 |

| 火 | **huǒ** fire (4 strokes) | **common words** 火把 **huǒbǎ** torch 火海 **huǒhǎi** a sea of flames 火车站 **huǒchēzhàn** train station | **radical** 火 |

| 车 | **chē** vehicle 車 Traditional (4 strokes) | **common words** 车库 **chēkù** garage 车速 **chēsù** vehicle speed 车水马龙 **chē shuǐ mǎlóng** (lit.) endless stream of horse and carriage; heavy traffic | **radical** 车 |

站	zhàn stand, station	common words		radical 立
(10 strokes)		站台　**zhàntái**　platform (at a railway station) 站票　**zhànpiào**　ticket for standing room 站得高，看得远　**zhàn dé gāo kàn dé yuǎn** 　　(lit.) stand high and see far; far-sighted		

丶	二	亠	立	立	站	站	站	站	站
站	站								

来	lái come	common words		radical 一
(7 strokes)	來 **Traditional**	来宾　**láibīn**　guest; visitor 来回　**láihuí**　make a round trip; return journey 来日方长　**láirì fāng cháng**　(idiom) the 　　future is long; there will be ample time		

一	丆	𠀆	𡗜	芉	来	来	来	来	来

去	qù go, past	common words		radical 土
(5 strokes)		去年　**qùnián**　last year 去留　**qùliú**　go or stay 去伪存真　**qùwěi cúnzhēn**　get rid of the 　　false and retain the true		

一	十	土	去	去	去	去	去		

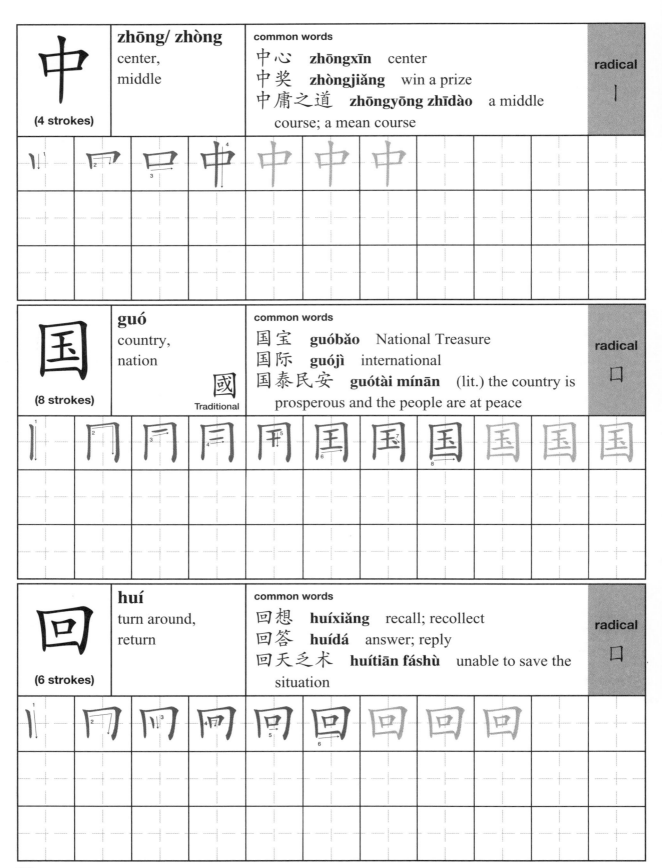

中

(4 strokes)

zhōng/ zhòng

center, middle

common words

中心　**zhōngxīn**　center

中奖　**zhòngjiǎng**　win a prize

中庸之道　**zhōngyōng zhīdào**　a middle course; a mean course

radical

丨

国

(8 strokes)

guó

country, nation

國

Traditional

common words

国宝　**guóbǎo**　National Treasure

国际　**guójì**　international

国泰民安　**guótài mínān**　(lit.) the country is prosperous and the people are at peace

radical

囗

回

(6 strokes)

huí

turn around, return

common words

回想　**huíxiǎng**　recall; recollect

回答　**huídá**　answer; reply

回天乏术　**huítiān fáshù**　unable to save the situation

radical

囗

北

běi

north

(5 strokes)

common words

北京　**běijīng**　Beijing
北欧　**běiōu**　North Europe
北美洲　**běiměi zhōu**　North America

radical

｜

丨	十	扌	北	北	北	北	北			

京

jīng

the capital
of a country

(8 strokes)

common words

京剧　**jīngjù**　Beijing opera
京腔　**jīngqiāng**　Beijing accent
京韵大鼓　**jīngyùn dàgǔ**　(lit.) story-telling in
Beijing dialect with drum accompaniment

radical

亠

丶	亠	亠	宀	立	宁	亰	京	京	京	京

坐

zuò

sit,
ride

(7 strokes)

common words

坐位　**zuòwèi**　seat
坐班　**zuòbān**　to work office hours
坐井观天　**zuòjǐng guāntiān**　(lit.) look at the
sky from the bottom of a well; narrow-minded

radical

土

亻	亽	亽丿	亽𠆢	坐	坐	坐	坐	坐	坐	

飞	**fēi** fly		**common words**		radical
(3 strokes)		飛 Traditional	飞机　**fēijī**　aircraft; plane 飞跑　**fēipǎo**　run like the wind 飞沙走石　**fēishā zǒushí**　(lit.) flying sand 　　and rolling pebbles		飞

飞	飞	飞	飞	飞	飞	飞				

机	**jī** machine, chance, plane		**common words**		radical
(6 strokes)		機 Traditional	机会　**jīhuì**　opportunity; chance 机场　**jīchǎng**　airport 机不可失　**jī bùkě shī**　(lit.) don't let such an 　　opportunity slip; no time to lose		木

一	十	才	木	机	机	机	机	机		

开	**kāi** open, bloom, turn on		**common words**		radical
(4 strokes)		開 Traditional	开门　**kāimén**　open the door 开心　**kāixīn**　happy; joyous 开天辟地　**kāitiān pìdì**　the creation of 　　heaven and earth; the beginning of history		一

一	二	开	开	开	开	开				

出	chū go out, exceed	**common words** 出差 **chūchāi** away on business trip 出国 **chūguó** go abroad 出租车 **chūzūchē** taxi	radical 凵
(5 strokes)			

凵	凵	屮	出	出	出	出	出			

租	zū rent, lease	**common words** 租车 **zūchē** rent a car 租房 **zūfáng** rent a room; rent a house 租金 **zūjīn** rental fee	radical 禾
(10 strokes)			

丿	二	千	禾	禾	利	和	和	租	租	租
租	租									

91

WORD PRACTICE

医院 **yīyuàn** hospital

医	院								

医生 **yīshēng** doctor

医	生								

工作 **gōngzuò** work, job

工	作								

火车站 **huǒchēzhàn** train station

火	车	站							

中国 **zhōngguó** China

中	国								

北京 **běijīng** Beijing

北	京								

飞机 **fēijī** air plane

飞	机								

出租车 **chūzūchē** taxi

出	租	车							

EXERCISE SET 9 • 练习九
He is Going to Beijing • 他要去北京

1. **Choose the correct word to complete the sentence. Each word can only be used once.**

中国	飞机	北京	学校	工作
火车站	出租车	医院	火车	看电影

1) 他要去 _____。

2) 她要去 _____。

3) 妈妈要去 _____。

4) 爸爸要去 _____。

5) 姐姐要去 _____。

6) 我朋友要去 _____。

7) 我要去 _____。

8) 她要坐 _____。

9) 他要坐 _____。

10) 我朋友要坐 _____。

2. **These characters 坐, 做, 作 have the same pinyin and tones but different meanings. Choose the right character to fill in the brackets.**

1) 你在（　　　）什么？我在看书。

2) 姐姐在（　　　）什么？姐姐在写字。

3) 你爸爸（　　　）什么工（　　　）？我爸爸是医生。

4) 你妈妈（　　　）什么工（　　　）？我妈妈是老师。

5) 你怎么去中国？我（　　　）飞机去中国。

6) 你怎么去北京？我（　　　）火车去北京。

7) 你怎么去学校？我（　　　）校车去学校。

8) 你怎么去火车站？我（　　　）出租车去火车站。

3. Fill in the space with the correct Chinese characters.

十	是	时	在	再

A.　现在（　　　　）点钟。

B.　现在（　　　　）什么（　　　　）候？

C.　这（　　　　）我学校。

D.　妈妈，（　　　　）见！

E.　我（　　　　）家里，不（　　　　）火车站。

4. Make your own sentences using the characters provided.

Example: 坐什么：爸爸坐什么车去北京？

1)　做　　：＿＿＿＿＿＿＿＿＿＿＿＿＿＿＿

2)　坐　　：＿＿＿＿＿＿＿＿＿＿＿＿＿＿＿

3)　工作　：＿＿＿＿＿＿＿＿＿＿＿＿＿＿＿

4)　我要去：＿＿＿＿＿＿＿＿＿＿＿＿＿＿＿

5)　他要回：＿＿＿＿＿＿＿＿＿＿＿＿＿＿＿

6)　她要坐：＿＿＿＿＿＿＿＿＿＿＿＿＿＿＿

7)　怎么去：＿＿＿＿＿＿＿＿＿＿＿＿＿＿＿

8)　怎么样：＿＿＿＿＿＿＿＿＿＿＿＿＿＿＿

5. Read the paragraph. Answer the questions using Chinese characters.

今天是星期三，天气很好，不冷不热。小明的爸爸要去北京开会。他要坐飞机去北京。从小明家坐飞机到北京要两个多小时，坐火车要十几个小时。小明的妈妈开车去工作。姐姐和小明坐校车去上学。星期六和星期天，姐姐和小明有时坐出租车去看电影。

1) 今天是星期几?天气怎么样?

_____

2) 小明的爸爸去北京做什么?

_____

3) 小明的爸爸怎么去北京?

_____

4) 小明的爸爸为什么不坐火车去北京?

_____

_____

5) 小明的妈妈怎么去上班?

_____

6) 姐姐和小明怎么去上学?

_____

7) 姐姐和小明怎么去看电影?

_____

商	**shāng** commerce, consult	common words 商人　**shāngrén**　businessman; merchant 商店　**shāngdiàn**　shop; store 商业区　**shāngyèqū**　business district; 　　　　　business area	radical 亠
(11 strokes)			

亠 亠 亠 亠 产 商 商 商 商 商 商

商 商 商

店	**diàn** shop, store	common words 店主　**diànzhǔ**　shop owner 店员　**diànyuán**　salesperson; shop assistant 店面　**diànmiàn**　shop front	radical 广
(8 strokes)			

亠 亠 广 广 庄 店 店 店 店 店

能	**néng** ability, capability	common words 能干　**nénggàn**　capable; competent 能够　**nénggòu**　can; be able to; be capable of 能上能下　**néngshàng néngxià**　be able to accept a higher or lower post	radical 厶
(10 strokes)			

厶 厶 台 育 育 育 育 能 能 能 能

能 能

买	**mǎi** buy, purchase 買 Traditional	**common words** 买书 **mǎishū** buy a book 买卖 **mǎimài** buying and selling; business 买椟还珠 **mǎidú huánzhū** (lit.) buy a wooden box and return the pearls inside; make a wrong choice	**radical** 一
(6 strokes)			

买 买 买 买 买 买 买 买 买

桌	**zhuō** table, desk	**common words** 桌子 **zhuōzi** table; desk 桌布 **zhuōbù** tablecloth 桌面上 **zhuōmiànshàng** on the table; (fig.) in public	**radical** 木
(10 strokes)			

桌 桌 桌 桌 桌 桌 桌 桌 桌 桌

桌 桌

椅	**yǐ** chair	**common words** 椅子 **yǐzi** chair 椅背 **yǐbèi** the back of a chair 椅套 **yǐtào** a slipcover for a chair	**radical** 木
(12 strokes)			

椅 椅 椅 椅 椅 椅 椅 椅 椅 椅 椅

椅 椅 椅 椅

衣	yī	common words	radical
(6 strokes)	clothing	衣料　**yīliào**　material for clothing 衣服　**yīfu**　clothes 衣冠楚楚　**yīguān chǔchǔ**　be immaculately 　　　　　dressed; well-groomed	衣

一　亠　亣　衣　衣　衣　衣　衣

服	fú	common words	radical
(8 strokes)	clothes, dress	服务　**fúwù**　serve; service 服装　**fúzhuāng**　dress; clothing; clothes 服服帖帖　**fú futiē tiē**　submissive; fitting; 　　　　　obedient	月

丿　刀　月　月　刖　服　服　服　服　服

会	huì/kuài	common words	radical
(6 strokes)	get together, meeting, can, be able to　會 　　　　Traditional	会议　**huìyì**　conference; meeting 会计　**kuàijì**　accountant, accountancy 会心会意　**huìxīn huìyì**　understanding; 　　　　　knowing	人

丿　人　仐　仝　会　会　会　会　会

多 (6 strokes)	duō many, much	**common words** 多次　**duōcì**　many times 多少　**duōshǎo**　how many; how much 多多益善　**duōduō yìshàn**　the more the better	radical 夕

少 (4 strokes)	shǎo few, little, **shào** young	**common words** 少有　**shǎoyǒu**　rare; a few 少年　**shàonián**　youngster 少见多怪　**shǎojiàn duōguài**　express excitement/surprise due to ignorance	radical 小

块 (7 strokes)	kuài a piece, a measure word 塊 Traditional	**common words** 一块　**yíkuài**　one piece; a piece 两块糖　**liǎngkuàitáng**　two pieces of candy 三块钱　**sānkuàiqián**　three dollars	radical 土

99

| 钱 (10 strokes) | **qián** money, coin, cash 錢 Traditional | **common words** 钱包 **qiánbāo** wallet; purse
钱币 **qiánbì** coin
钱迷心窍 **qiánmí xīnqiào** be blinded by lust for money | **radical** 钅 |

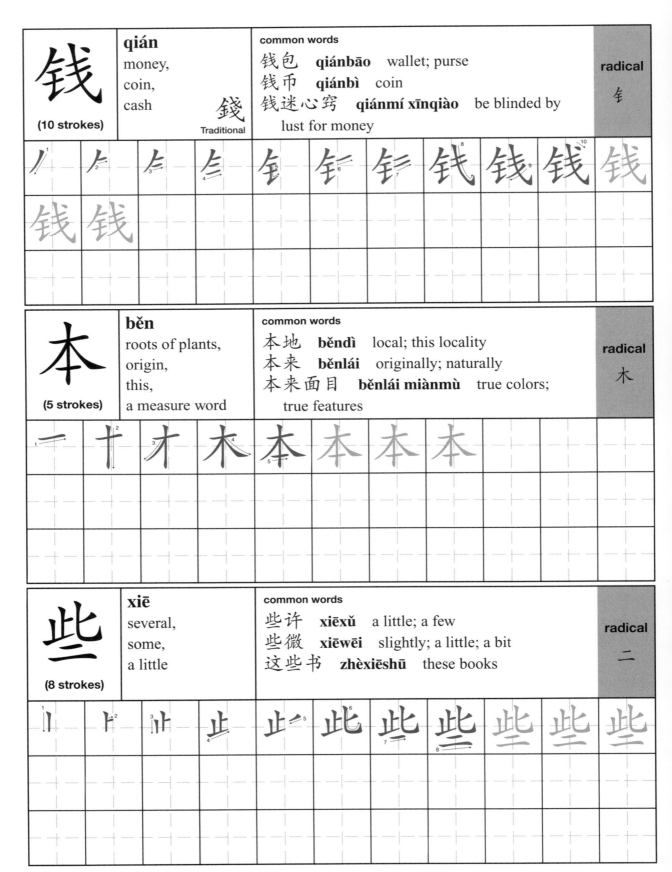

| 本 (5 strokes) | **běn** roots of plants, origin, this, a measure word | **common words** 本地 **běndì** local; this locality
本来 **běnlái** originally; naturally
本来面目 **běnlái miànmù** true colors; true features | **radical** 木 |

| 些 (8 strokes) | **xiē** several, some, a little | **common words** 些许 **xiēxǔ** a little; a few
些微 **xiēwēi** slightly; a little; a bit
这些书 **zhèxiēshū** these books | **radical** 二 |

商店　**shāngdiàn**　shop, store

商	店								

桌子　**zhuōzi**　table, desk

桌	子								

椅子　**yǐzi**　chair

椅	子								

衣服　**yīfu**　clothes

衣	服								

多少　**duōshǎo**　how many, how much

多	少								

EXERCISE SET 10 • 练习十
Let's Go Shopping! • 走,买东西去!

1. **Rewrite the words in Chinese characters.**

1)　store　(　　)　2)　table　　　　　(　　)

3)　chair　(　　)　4)　clothing　　　(　　)

5)　book　(　　)　6)　book store　　(　　)

7)　to buy　　（　　　）　8)　to sell　　　　　　（　　　）

9)　money　（　　　）　10)　how much (many)　（　　　）

2. Read the questions. Rewrite the answer in Chinese characters.

1)　A:　妈妈和你去商店吗？

　　B:　We will go to the store.

　　_____

2)　A:　你们怎么去商店？

　　B:　We will drive to the store.

　　_____

3)　A:　你有那本书吗？

　　B:　I don't have that book.

　　_____

4)　A:　你要买那本书吗？

　　B:　I will buy that book.

　　_____

5)　A:　你买桌子吗？

　　B:　I will not buy a table.

　　_____

6)　A:　他会不会写中国字？

　　B:　He is able to write Chinese characters.

　　_____

7) A: 你爸爸坐不坐飞机？
    B: My father doesn't take the airplane.

    _____

8) A: 你姐姐的中文怎么样？
    B: My older sister's Chinese is very good.

    _____

3. **Make your own sentences using the characters provided.**

    Example: 买 ： 哥哥买了很多书。

    1) 什么   ： _____

    2) 不   ： _____

    3) 多少   ： _____

    4) 多少钱 ： _____

    5) 多少本 ： _____

    6) 会   ： _____

    7) 不会   ： _____

    8) 会不会 ： _____

    9) 坐不坐 ： _____

    10) 去书店 ： _____

4. Fill in the spaces with the appropriate words.

商店	电脑	四本书	椅子
天气	桌子	电视机	也去了

今天（   ）很好，妈妈和我去（   ）买东西。
我们买了（   ）,（   ）,（   ）和（   ）。
我们（   ）书店。妈妈买了（   ）。我买了三本书。

5. Rewrite the sentences in Chinese Characters.

1) Today is Saturday. My mother and I go to the store to buy something.

_____

2) Xiǎo Míng went to the book store and bought a lot of books yesterday.

_____

3) My father bought one computer.

_____

4) I go to the store to buy some clothes. The store has a lot of people.

_____

5) My older sister wants to buy a small table.

_____

6) I don't want to buy a table, I want to buy a chair.

_____

米	**mǐ** rice	**common words**		radical
(6 strokes)		米饭　**mǐfàn**　rice 米糕　**mǐgāo**　rice cake 米粮川　**mǐliángchuān**　rich rice producing 　　　area		米

丶	丷	半	半	米	米	米	米	米		

饭	**fàn** meal, cooked rice 飯 Traditional	**common words**		radical
(7 strokes)		饭店　**fàndiàn**　restaurant; hotel 饭厅　**fàntīng**　dining hall 饭馆　**fànguǎn**　restaurant		饣

丿	𠂉	饣	饣	饭	饭	饭	饭	饭	饭		

菜	**cài** vegetables 菜 Traditional	**common words**		radical
(11 strokes)		菜园　**càiyuán**　vegetable garden 菜油　**càiyóu**　vegetable oil 蔬菜　**shūcài**　vegetables		艹

一	十	艹	艹	艹	苎	芝	荢	荜	莁	菜
菜	菜	菜								

水	**shuǐ** water	**common words**		radical
(4 strokes)		水果　**shuǐguǒ**　fruits 水库　**shuǐkù**　reservoir 水天一色　**shuǐtiān yísè**　the sea and the sky 　merged in one color; the beauty of nature		水

丿	刁	水	水	水	水	水			

苹	**píng** apple	**common words**		radical
(8 strokes)	蘋 **Traditional**	苹果　**píngguǒ**　apple 苹果汁　**píngguǒzhī**　apple juice 苹果手机　**píngguǒ shǒujī**　iphone		艹

一	十	艹	艾	芇	芇	莁	苹	苹	苹	苹

果	**guǒ** fruit, result, consequence	**common words**		radical
(8 strokes)		果冻　**guǒdòng**　jelly 果汁　**guǒzhī**　fruit juice 果不其然　**guǒ bù qí rán**　sure enough; 　just as expected		木

丶	冂	曰	旦	旦	甲	畀	果	果	果	果

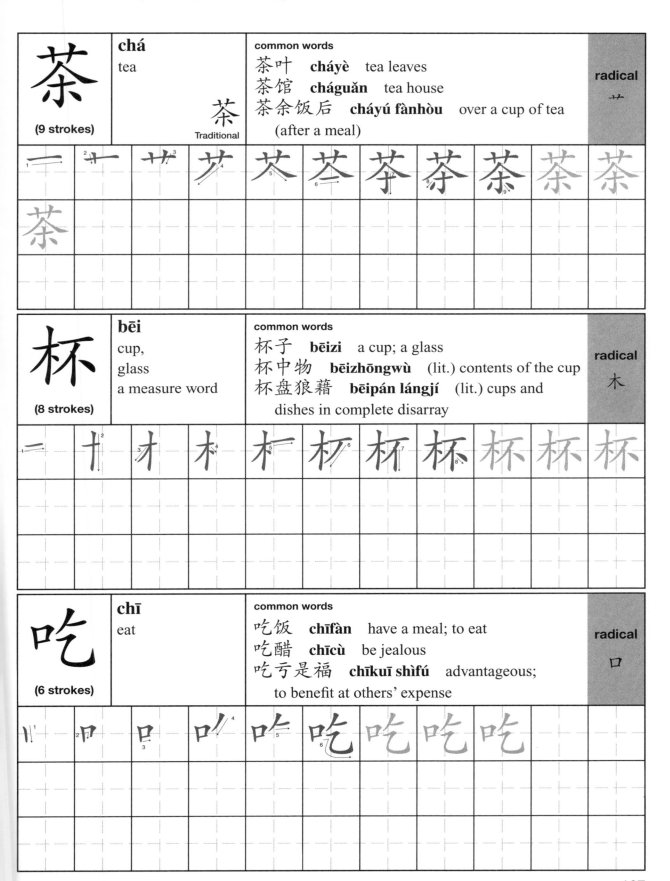

茶

chá
tea

(9 strokes)

茶 Traditional

common words

茶叶　**cháyè**　tea leaves
茶馆　**cháguǎn**　tea house
茶余饭后　**cháyú fànhòu**　over a cup of tea
(after a meal)

radical
艹

杯

bēi
cup,
glass
a measure word

(8 strokes)

common words

杯子　**bēizi**　a cup; a glass
杯中物　**bēizhōngwù**　(lit.) contents of the cup
杯盘狼藉　**bēipán lángjí**　(lit.) cups and
dishes in complete disarray

radical
木

吃

chī
eat

(6 strokes)

common words

吃饭　**chīfàn**　have a meal; to eat
吃醋　**chīcù**　be jealous
吃亏是福　**chīkuī shìfú**　advantageous;
to benefit at others' expense

radical
口

| 喝 (12 strokes) | **hē/hè** drink | common words 喝茶　**hēchá**　drink tea 喝彩　**hècǎi**　acclaim; cheer; applause 喝西北风　**hē xīběifēng**　(lit.) drink the northwest wind; (fig.) cold and hungry | radical 口 |

丨	口	口	口	吗	唱	喟	吗	喝	喝	喝
喝	喝	喝	喝							

| 馆 (11 strokes) | **guǎn** place for cultural activities, building 館 Traditional | common words 旅馆　**lǚguǎn**　hotel; motel 图书馆　**túshūguǎn**　library 博物馆　**bówùguǎn**　museum | radical 饣 |

丿	𠂊	饣	饣	饣	饣	馆	馆	馆	馆	馆
馆	馆	馆								

WORD PRACTICE

米饭 **mǐfàn** rice

米	饭								

饭馆 **fànguǎn** restaurant

饭	馆								

水果 **shuǐguǒ** fruits

水	果								

苹果 **píngguǒ** apple

苹	果								

杯子 **bēizi** cup

杯	子								

1. Match the pinyin to the Chinese characters.

mǐfàn	píngguǒ	shuǐguǒ	hēshuǐ	bēizī
水果	米饭	喝水	杯子	苹果

2. Read the question. Rewrite the answer in Chinese characters.

1) 你喜欢吃什么饭？

I like to eat rice.

_____

2) 他喜欢吃什么水果？

He likes to eat apple.

_____

3) 妈妈喜欢喝什么？

Mother likes to drink tea.

_____

4) 爸爸喜欢喝什么？

Father likes to drink water.

_____

5) 这是中国饭馆吗？

Yes, this is a Chinese restaurant.

_____

6) 那是北京茶馆吗？

No, that is not a Beijing tea house.

_____

3. Make your own sentences using the characters provided.

Example: 喝茶 ： 我们去茶馆喝茶，好吗？

1) 吃 ： _____

2) 吃什么 ： _____

3) 喝 ： _____

4) 喝什么 ： _____

5) 喜欢 ： _____

6) 不喜欢 ： _____

7) 很喜欢 ： _____

8) 高兴 ： _____

4. Read the dialog. Answer the questions in Chinese characters.

小明 ： 东东，你要去哪里？

东东 ： 我要去商店。

小明 ： 你要买什么？

东东 ： 我要买水果和菜。

小明 ： 你要买什么水果？

东东 ： 我要买苹果。

小明 ： 你喜欢吃苹果吗？

东东 ： 我喜欢，你呢？

小明 ： 我也很喜欢吃苹果。

1) 东东要去哪里？

   _____

2) 东东要买什么？

   _____

3) 东东喜欢吃什么水果？

   _____

4) 小明喜欢吃什么水果？

   _____

5. **Read and copy these Chinese phrases.**

吃不吃	_____	喝不喝	_____
是不是	_____	去不去	_____
在不在	_____	买不买	_____
会不会	_____	好不好	_____
看不看	_____	听不听	_____
说不说	_____	读不读	_____
写不写	_____	有没有	_____
喜欢不喜欢	_____	高兴不高兴	_____

6. Fill in the brackets with the appropriate words.

火车	天气	三本书	喜欢	买了
中国菜	午饭	喝茶	学校	米饭

今天是星期天，（　　　　　）很好。上午，小明和他的朋友们坐（　　　　　）到北京去玩。他们到商店（　　　　　）一些东西。他们也去了书店，买了（　　　　　）。他们还去了中国饭馆吃（　　　　　）。他们要了好几个（　　　　　）和米饭。小明和他的朋友都很（　　　　　）吃中国菜和（　　　　　）。吃完饭，他们又去茶馆（　　　　　）。下午，他们坐火车回到（　　　　　）。

| 爱 (10 strokes) | **ài** love, be fond of / 愛 **Traditional** | **common words** 爱情 **àiqíng** romance (between man and woman) 爱国 **àiguó** love one's country; patriotic 爱不释手 **ài bú shìshǒu** love something so much that one would not let it out of one's hand | **radical** ⺤(爪) |

| 喜 (12 strokes) | **xǐ** like | **common words** 喜欢 **xǐhuan** like 喜悦 **xǐyuè** happy; joyous 喜气洋洋 **xǐqì yángyáng** full of joy; jubilant | **radical** 口 |

| 欢 (6 strokes) | **huān** joyous, merry, jubilant / 歡 **Traditional** | **common words** 欢呼 **huānhū** hail; cheers 欢迎 **huānyíng** welcome; greeting 欢天喜地 **huān tiān xǐ dì** with boundless joy; delighted | **radical** 又 |

猫	**māo** cat		**common words**		radical 犭
(11 strokes)	貓 **Traditional**		猫眼　**māoyǎn**　peephole; spyhole 猫头鹰　**māotóuyīng**　owl 猫哭耗子　**māo kū hàozi**　(idiom) the cat weeps for the dead mouse; crocodile tears		

ノ	丬	犭	犭一	犭⁺	犭⁺⁺	猫	猫	猫	猫	猫
猫	猫	猫								

狗	**gǒu** dog		**common words**		radical 犭
(8 strokes)			狗牙　**gǒuyá**　dog tooth 狗皮　**gǒupí**　dog skin 狗急跳墙　**gǒují tiàoqiáng**　(idiom) a desperate dog will jump over the wall; to be driven to desperate action		

ノ	丬	犭	犭	狗	狗	狗	狗	狗	狗	狗

想	**xiǎng** think, want to		**common words**		radical 心
(13 strokes)			想法　**xiǎngfǎ**　idea; opinion 想念　**xiǎngniàn**　miss; thinking about 想入非非　**xiǎngrù fēifēi**　(idiom) to indulge in fantasy; letting one's imagination run wild		

一	十	才	木	相	相	相	相	相	相	想
想	想	想	想	想						

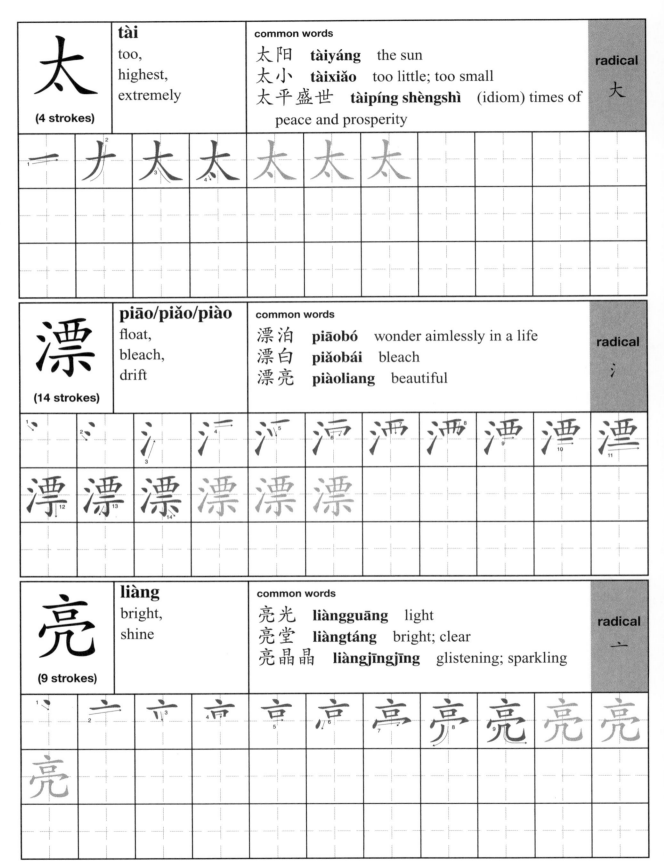

太 (4 strokes)

tài
too,
highest,
extremely

common words

太阳　**tàiyáng**　the sun
太小　**tàixiǎo**　too little; too small
太平盛世　**tàipíng shèngshì**　(idiom) times of
peace and prosperity

radical
大

漂 (14 strokes)

piāo/piǎo/piào
float,
bleach,
drift

common words

漂泊　**piāobó**　wonder aimlessly in a life
漂白　**piǎobái**　bleach
漂亮　**piàoliang**　beautiful

radical
氵

亮 (9 strokes)

liàng
bright,
shine

common words

亮光　**liàngguāng**　light
亮堂　**liàngtáng**　bright; clear
亮晶晶　**liàngjīngjīng**　glistening; sparkling

radical
亠

| 都 (10 strokes) | **dōu/dū** all, entire | **common words** 都有 **dōuyǒu** have it all
都市 **dūshì** city; metropolis
都不知道 **dōu bùzhīdào** no one knows; don't know at all | radical 阝 |

| 一 | 十 | 土 | 耂 | 才 | 者 | 者 | 者 | 都 | 都 | 都 |
| 都 | 都 | | | | | | | | | |

| 睡 (13 strokes) | **shuì** sleep | **common words** 睡衣 **shuìyī** pajamas
睡袋 **shuìdài** sleeping bag
睡眼惺忪 **shuìyǎn xīngsōng** have a drowsy look | radical 目 |

| 丨 | 冂 | 月 | 月 | 目 | 目 | 盱 | 盱 | 眍 | 眍 | 眍 |
| 睡 | 睡 | 睡 | 睡 | 睡 | | | | | | |

| 觉 (9 strokes) | **jué/jiào** feel, sense, sleep
覺 Traditional | **common words** 觉得 **juéde** feel; sense
睡觉 **shuìjiào** sleep
一觉醒来 **yījiào xǐnglái** wake up from a sleep | radical 见 |

| 丷 | 丷 | 丷 | 丷 | 丷 | 尚 | 觉 | 觉 | 觉 | 觉 | 觉 |
| 觉 | | | | | | | | | | |

WORD PRACTICE

喜欢 **xǐhuan** like

喜	欢								

睡觉 **shuìjiào** sleep

睡	觉								

漂亮 **piàoliang** beautiful

漂	亮								

EXERCISE SET 12 • 练习十二
He Loves His Dog!• 他很爱他的小狗!

1. **Identify the characters with the same radicals. Write them in the spaces provided.**

狗	样	吃	他	她	明	认	天	呢
校	妈	识	昨	听	汉	再	好	大
喝	你	猫	吗	上	机	什	话	姐
们	桌	时	作	语	下	哪	日	谁
谢	叫	东	果	候	读	没	住	开
杯	本	漂	来	面	喂	椅	做	说

一： _____, _____, _____, _____, _____, _____, _____,

_____, _____, _____

犭： _____, _____

讠： _____, _____, _____, _____, _____, _____, _____

_____

亻： _____, _____, _____, _____, _____, _____, _____

_____

女： _____, _____, _____, _____

氵： _____, _____, _____

口： _____, _____, _____, _____, _____, _____, _____,

_____

日： _____, _____, _____, _____

木： _____, _____, _____, _____, _____, _____, _____

2. Fill in the blanks using Chinese characters.

1) 我们都很_____(love) 我们的爸爸和妈妈。

2) 小明很_____(like) 他的大狗和小猫。

3) 东东晚上九点钟_____(go to bed)。

4) 小明的姐姐_____(very beautiful)。

3. Make your own sentences using the characters provided.

Example: 很爱： 他很爱他的爸爸和妈妈。

1) 爱 ： _____

2) 喜欢 : _____

3) 想   : _____

4) 都想 : _____

4. Read and copy these Chinese phrases.

太大了 （   ） 太小了 （   ）

太热了 （   ） 太冷了 （   ）

太多了 （   ） 太少了 （   ）

太好吃了（   ）太好喝了 （   ）

太高兴了（   ）太喜欢了 （   ）

太爱她了（   ）太想他了 （   ）

5. Rewrite the sentences in Chinese characters.

1) I love my small dog very much. I don't like cat.

    _____

2) He goes to bed at 9:00 o'clock every night.

    _____

3) We all miss our older sister and she also misses us.

    _____

4) She is my good friend. She is beautiful and is also a good student.

    _____

Answer Key

Exercise Set 1

1 一; 二; 三; 四; 五; 六; 七; 八; 九; 十; 零

2 shíwǔ 十五; èrshíèr 二十二; sānshíqī 三十七; shíjiǔ 十九; liùshíbā 六十八; qīshíyī 七十一; bāshísì 八十四

3 6; 7; 3; 9; 5; 4; 8; 10; 007; 52; 83; 99; 44; 55; 77; 88; 66; 12; 31; 76

4 twelve—十二; fourteen—十四; twenty six—二十六; thirty one—三十一; forty eight—四十八; fifty six—五十六; sixty five—六十五; seventy three—七十三; eighty nine—八十九; ninety two—九十二

Exercise Set 2

1 好; 很好; 我; 我们; 你; 你们; 他; 他们; 她; 她们; 叫; 名字

2 1) 你好吗？我很好，你呢？　2) 你叫什么名字？
3) 他（她）叫什么名字？　4) 很高兴认识你。

3 你; 他; 们; 什／她; 好／吗; 呢; 叫

4 他; 认; 很; 名; 字

5 高兴; 认识; 很好; 我们; 什么; 名字; 你呢

6 1) 你叫什么名字？　2) 你认识她吗？　3) 他很高兴。　4) 很高兴认识你。

7 1) 你好吗？　2) 我很好，你呢？　3) 很高兴认识你。

Exercise Set 3

1 nǐ—你; zài—再; méi—没; xiè—谢; kè—客; guān—关; qǐ—起; xì—系; jiàn—见; qì—气

2 1) 你们好！　2) 我很好，谢谢！　3) 没关系，不客气！　4) 谢谢你们！
5) 我们很高兴。

3 谢谢; 不客气; 对不起; 没关系

4 吗; 很好; 呢; 认识; 不客气; 再见

Exercise Set 4

1 1) 星期一　2) 十一月五号　3) 星期六　4) 星期日　5) 十二月七号

2 1A) 明天是星期五吗？　2A) 今天是三月十号吗？　3B) 是的，昨天是星期四。
4B) 现在是下午三点二十四分。

3 三，七，六; 三，八，天; 明，三，五月十一号，一; 九，八，星期三，九，七，星期二

4 五点钟; 五点五十分; 六点十分

5 1) 今天是星期几？今天是星期一。　2) 昨天是星期几？昨天是星期天。
3) 明天是星期几？明天是星期二。　4) 今天是七月十五号吗？是，今天是七月十五号。

5) 昨天是八月六号吗？不是，昨天是八月七号。

6) 明天是十二月一号吗？是，明天是十二月一号。

7) 现在是几点？现在是六点三十分 / 六点三十。

8) 现在是十二点十分吗？不，不是，是十二点五分。

9) 现在是上午十一点二十分 / 十一点二十。

10) 现在是下午三点吗？是，是下午三点。

Exercise Set 5

1 jīn; tiān; míng; xià; shén; lěng; jǐ; zěn; kè; xì

2 1) 天气 2) 雨 3) 热 4) 看见 5) 刮风

3 天气，天天，天热，天冷；今天；很热，很冷；怎么；刮风；下雨；明天

5 1) 今天下午会刮风吗？ 2) 星期五上午会下雨。 3) 今天天气很热。

4) 明天下午天气怎么样？ 5) 昨天上午很冷。 6) 今天下午不热。

7) 明天不会刮大风。 8) 你看见下雨了吗？

7 今天是星期天。现在是早上七点。今天天气怎么样？今天天气不好，很冷，会刮大风和下雨。

8 1) Yesterday was Saturday. How was the weather yesterday? Yesterday was very hot.

2) How is the weather today? Today is very cold, it will be windy and raining. Today's weather is not very good.

3) How is the weather going to be tomorrow? Tomorrow's weather will be very good, not cold and not hot, not windy and not raining.

Exercise Set 6

2 亻—你, 们, 他, 什, 做,

讠—认, 识, 说, 话, 读, 请, 谢

木—样, 校

口—听, 叫, 吗, 呢

3 1) 看书, 看电视 2) 写字, 写书 3) 学汉语, 打电话

5 你天天看书。；老师天天去学校。；学生天天读书。；我天天学汉语。；她天天写汉字
我们在看电影。；学生们在学习。；我同学在看电视。；老师们在学校。；他们在看书。

Exercise Set 7

1 father—bàba—爸爸; old sister—jiějie—姐姐; son—érzi—儿子; mother—māma—妈妈; daughter—nǚer—女儿; husband—xiānsheng—先生; doctor—yīshēng—医生; teacher—lǎoshī—老师; miss—xiǎojiě—小姐; student—xuéshēng—学生

2 1) 我的爸爸, 我的妈妈, 我的姐姐 2) 我的家, 我女儿的家, 我儿子的家

3) 有四个人, 有两个人, 有三个人 4) 十七岁, 二十一岁, 十八岁

4 1) 妈妈 2) 女儿 3) 爸爸 4) 先生 5) 这是 6) 那是 7) 小姐

   8) 学生 9) 怎么样 10) 天气 11) 我家 12) 下雨 13) 儿子

5 我家(有)四个人, 爸爸, 妈妈, 姐姐和我。今天是 (星期天)。天气很冷, (在下雨),

   我们都在(家)里。我的爸爸和妈妈都是(老师)。姐姐是(大学生), 我是(小学生)。

   现在, 我的爸爸和妈妈在(看书), 姐姐在(学汉语), 我在(打)电话。

Exercise Set 8

1 nǎr; nǎlǐ; zhèr; zhèlǐ; nàr; nàlǐ; qián; qiǎnmiàn; hòu; hòumiàn; lǐ; lǐmiàn

3 1) 今天是星期六。 2) 东东在家里。 3) 东东在家里看书。

   4) 小明和东东要去看电影。 5) 电影是下午四点钟。

4 口—哪, 听, 喂, 呢; 亻—住, 做, 什; 讠—说, 话, 读

5 1) 爸爸在学校。 2) 妈妈在家里。 3) 姐姐在那儿。 4) 我在这儿。

   5) 你朋友在那里。

   1) 电话在家里。 2) 电脑在这里。 3) 书在电脑前面。 4) 电视在那里。

   5) 那个东西在电视后面。

6 1) 你朋友在哪里? 她在学校。 2) 那个人是谁? 他是我同学。

   3) 你住在哪儿? 我家在我学校后面。 4) 你的姐姐在哪儿? 她在那儿。

Exercise Set 9

1 1) 中国 2) 火车站 3) 工作 4) 北京 5) 医院 6) 看电影 7) 学校

   8) 火车 9) 飞机 10) 出租车

2 1) 你在 (做) 什么? 2) 姐姐在 (做) 什么? 3) 你爸爸 (做) 什么工 (作)?

   4) 你妈妈 (做) 什么工 (作)? 5) 我 (坐)飞机去中国。 6) 我 (坐) 火车去北京。

   7) 我 (坐) 校车去学校。 8) 我 (坐) 出租车去火车站。

3 A. 现在 (十) 点钟。 B. 现在 (是) 什么 (时) 候?

   C. 这 (是) 我学校。 D. 妈妈,(再) 见! E. 我 (在) 家里, 不 (在) 火车站。

5 1) 今天是星期三。天气很好。 2) 小明的爸爸去北京开会。

   3) 小明的爸爸坐飞机去北京。 4) 坐火车去北京要十几个小时, 坐飞机才两个多小时。

   5) 小明的妈妈开车去上班。 6) 姐姐和小明坐校车去上学。

   7) 姐姐和小明坐出租车去看电影。

Exercise Set 10

1 1) 商店 2) 桌子 3) 椅子 4) 衣服 5) 书 6) 书店 7) 买 8) 卖 9) 钱 10) 多少

2 1) 我们要去商店。 2) 我们开车去商店。 3) 我没有那本书。 4) 我要买那本书。

   5) 我不买桌子。 6) 他会写中国字。 7) 我爸爸不坐飞机。 8) 我姐姐的中文很好。

4 今天 (天气)很好, 妈妈和我去 (商店)买东西。我们买了 (桌子), (椅子), (电脑)

   和 (电视机)。我们 (也去了) 书店。妈妈买了 (四本书)。我买了三本书。

5 1) 今天是星期六。我妈妈和我去商店买东西。 2) 小明昨天去书店买了很多书。

   3) 我爸爸买了一个电脑。 4) 我去商店买衣服。商店里有很多人。

5) 我姐姐要买小桌子。　　6) 我不要买桌子，我要买椅子。

Exercise Set 11

1　mǐfàn—米饭；píngguǒ—苹果；shuǐguǒ—水果；hēshuǐ—喝水；bēizī—杯子

2　1) 我喜欢吃米饭。　　2) 他喜欢吃苹果。　　3) 妈妈喜欢喝茶。　　4) 爸爸喜欢喝水。

　　5) 是的，这是中国饭馆。　　6) 不是，那不是北京茶馆。

4　1) 东东要去商店。　　2) 东东要买水果和菜。

　　3) 东东喜欢吃苹果。　　4) 小明也很喜欢吃苹果。

6　今天是星期天，(天气) 很好。上午，小明和他的朋友们坐 (火车) 到北京去玩。

　　他们到商店 (买了) 一些东西。他们也去了书店，买了 (三本书)。他们还去了

　　中国饭馆吃 (午饭)。他们要了好几个 (中国菜) 和米饭。小明和他的朋友都很

　　(喜欢) 吃中国菜和 (米饭)。吃完饭，他们又去茶馆 (喝茶)。下午，他们坐火车回到 (学校)。

Exercise Set 12

1　一—天，大，再，面，东，来，本，开，上，下；犭—狗，猫；讠—认，识，语，谁，谢，读 ，说，话；

　　亻—他，你，们，什，作，候，住，做；女—她，妈，好，姐；氵—汉，漂，没；

　　口—吃，喝，叫，呢，吗，哪，听，喂；日—日，明，昨，时；木—样，校，杯，机，桌，椅，果

2　1) 爱　　2) 喜欢　　3) 睡觉　　4) 很漂亮

5　1) 我很爱我的小狗。我不喜欢猫。　　2) 他每天晚上九点钟睡觉。

　　3) 我们都很想我们的姐姐，她也很想我们。

　　4) 她是我的好朋友。她很漂亮，也是一个好学生。

English–Chinese Index

A

a measure word, 个 **gè** 68
a particle 的 **de** 71
a piece, a measure word 块 **kuài** 99
ability, capability 能 **néng** 96
above, go up 上 **shàng** 36
again, once more, further 再 **zài** 30
air, gas 气 **qì** 27
all, entire 都 **dōu** 117
and, harmony, sum 和 **hé** 70
appearance, shape 样 **yàng** 47
apple 苹 **píng** 106

B

behind, back, later 后 **hòu** 78
below, under, next 下 **xià** 36
big, large 大 **dà** 68
bleach 漂 **piǎo** 116
book, to write, document 书 **shū** 55
brain 脑 **nǎo** 56
bright 明 **míng** 35
bright, shine 亮 **liàng** 116
buy, purchase 买 **mǎi** 97

C

call, shout 叫 **jiào** 19
capital of a country 京 **jīng** 89
cat 猫 **māo** 115
center, middle 中 **zhōng** 88
chair 椅 **yǐ** 97
character, word 字 **zì** 20
child, a suffix 儿 **ér** 65
Chinese 汉 **hàn** 55
clock, bell 钟 **zhōng** 34
clothing 衣 **yī** 98
clothes, dress 服 **fú** 98
cold 冷 **lěng** 45
come 来 **lái** 87
commence, consult 商 **shāng** 96
country, nation 国 **guó** 88

courtyard, institution 院 **yuàn** 85
cup, glass, a measure word 杯 **bēi** 107
cure, treat 医 **yī** 85
current, present 现 **xiàn** 39

D

day, sky 天 **tiān** 36
day 日 **rì** 38
do, make, produce 做 **zuò** 53
do not have, without 没 **méi** 29
dog 狗 **gǒu** 115
dot, o'clock, point 点 **diǎn** 34
drink 喝 **hē** 108

E

earlier, before, prior 先 **xiān** 66
east 东 **dōng** 79
eat 吃 **chī** 107
eight 八 **bā** 13
electricity, electronic 电 **diàn** 56
exist, be, at, be alive 在 **zài** 39

F

face, surface, top 面 **miàn** 79
father 爸 **bà** 64
feel, sense 觉 **jué** 117
female 女 **nǚ** 65
few, little 少 **shǎo** 99
fire 火 **huǒ** 86
five 五 **wǔ** 12
float, drift 漂 **piāo/piào** 116
fly 飞 **fēi** 90
four 四 **sì** 12
friend 朋 **péng** 77; 友 **yǒu** 77
front, ahead, forward 前 **qián** 78
fruit, result, consequence 果 **guǒ** 106

G

get together, meeting, can, be able to 会 **huì** 98
get up, rise, begin 起 **qǐ** 28
go, past 去 **qù** 87
go out, exceed 出 **chū** 91
good 好 **hǎo** 19
guest, visitor 客 **kè** 27

H

have, has 有 **yǒu** 70
he 他 **tā** 17
hello, hey, to feed 喂 **wèi** 77
high, tall 高 **gāo** 21
hit, beat 打 **dǎ** 54
home, family 家 **jiā** 64
hot, heat 热 **rè** 45
how, why 怎 **zěn** 46

I

I, me 我 **wǒ** 17
inside, in, within 里 **lǐ** 79
interrogative particle 么 **me** 20

J

joyous, merry, jubilant 欢 **huān** 114

K

know 识 **shí** 22

L

language 语 **yǔ** 55
like 喜 **xǐ** 114
listen, hear 听 **tīng** 53
live, stay 住 **zhù** 71
love, be fond of 爱 **ài** 114

M

machine, chance, plane 机 **jī** 90
meal, cooked rice 饭 **fàn** 105
minutes (time), divide 分 **fēn** 34

125

Hanyu Pinyin Index